IMAGES
of America

BLACK
ATLANTA
IN THE ROARING TWENTIES

Langston Hughes

Cover photograph: The J. Neal Montgomery Combo, one of the bands who entertained Black Atlantans during the 1920s at the Roof Garden on top of the Odd Fellows Building on Auburn Avenue (*c.* 1923), pose for this photograph at the studio of photographer Paul Poole.

IMAGES
of America

BLACK
ATLANTA
IN THE ROARING TWENTIES

Herman "Skip" Mason, Jr.

ARCADIA

First published 1997
Copyright © Herman "Skip" Mason, Jr., 1997

ISBN 0-7524-0887-9

Published by Arcadia Publishing,
an imprint of the Chalford Publishing Corporation,
One Washington Center, Dover, New Hampshire 03820.
Printed in Great Britain

Library of Congress Cataloging-in-Publication Data applied for

*To my first teacher, my mother,
and to the the teachers of Berea Academy,
E.C. Clement, G.A. Towns, and Ben Hill Elementary Schools and
D.M. Therrell High School,
who encouraged my love of reading and my interest in history.*

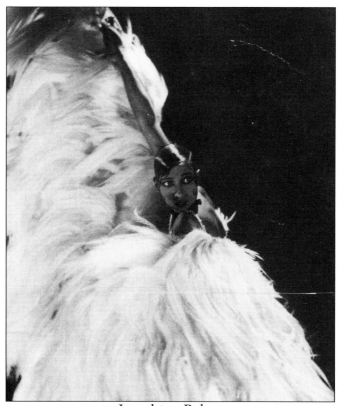

Josephine Baker

Contents

Introduction

"... We have within us as a race new stirrings, stirrings of the beginning of a new appreciation of joy, of a new will to be, as though in this morning of life we had awakened from some sleep that at once dimly mourns the past and dreams a splendid future."

W.E.B. DuBois
The Crisis, 1926

Why a picture book on Black Atlanta in the 1920s? Why not? While Harlem residents were enjoying their celebrated renaissance, African Americans in Atlanta were reveling in their own rebirth. As New Yorkers were experiencing a rebirth in culture and arts, blacks in Atlanta were experiencing an era of social and political awakening. These collected images in this book provide a glimpse at some of the personalities and institutions in Atlanta during this era. Atlanta was no Harlem, but then Harlem was no Atlanta.

The first year of the new decade found African Americans in Atlanta still readjusting from the Great Fire of 1917. The fire, which took place on May 21,1917, displaced ten thousand people and destroyed over 1,900 homes at a property loss of $5.5 million. While it destroyed much of the Old Fourth Ward, the business district of Auburn Avenue was spared.

Fathers and sons returned gallantly from World War One in 1918. The outcry of the Red Summer of 1919, where racial riots broke out throughout the country, still echoed in the minds of many. Despite these atrocities, the decade of the 1920s brought about a great sense of promise and hope for the city of Atlanta and its African-American population.

The previous decade in Atlanta had been one of great accomplishments for African Americans. The Odd Fellows Fraternal Organization, through the leadership of fellow member and fiery editor of the *Independent* and outspoken advocate for humanity Benjamin Davis, constructed two buildings, a six-floor office building, and 1,300-seat auditorium in 1912 and 1914 respectively. The Women's Branch YWCA was formed at the Blue Triangle Center on Piedmont Avenue on September 4, 1919, and at the suggestion of Selena Sloan Butler, it was named for Phyllis Wheatley. The first membership drive in 1922 was successful, reaching its goal of raising $2,000. The Southern Field Division of the National Urban League was organized in 1920, and the Atlanta Black Crackers Negro League baseball team was formed. The city also saw its first class of African-American nurses graduate from the Grady Hospital Training School during this decade.

In Harlem, the atmosphere was different. Entertainment dominated the twenties. There was the Lafayette and the Apollo Theaters which provided vaudeville and moving pictures. The entertainment options for black Atlantans included the Sunset Casino and Amusement Park and movie houses such as the Crystal on Hunter Street, the Paramount (later renamed the Royal) in the Odd Fellows Auditorium, and vaudeville performances at the infamous 81 and 91 Theaters on Decatur Street, Atlanta's version of the Apollo. It was at the 81 Theater where a young Thomas Dorsey, known as "Georgia Tom," played the piano and sang with Gertrude Rainey, known professionally as "Ma Rainey," and her Black Bottom band. It was also at the 81 Theater where Ethel Waters, Bessie Smith, Butterbeans and Susie, the Whitman Sisters, and hundreds of others blues singers, musicians, and vaudeville performers on the Theater Owners Booking Association circuit played. And yes, silent movies, accompanied by the strains of the pump organ played by Graham Jackson, were seen daily at the 81 and the Crystal Theaters. At the end of the decade in 1929, Big Bethel AME Church member Lula Byrd Jones presented the idea for a pageant titled *Heaven Bound,* which was to become a cultural landmark and yearly tradition for Atlantans.

There was 125th Street in Harlem and Decatur Street in Atlanta. Both streets were segregated, energetic, risqué, and full of color. It was on those streets where African Americans could be found in the barbershops, brothels, restaurants, cafes, juke joints, and night clubs. Scents of fried fish and chicken prevailed, along with blaring lights and the illegal sale of moonshine and whiskey.

One Atlantan recalled in the book *Living Atlanta: An Oral History*, "that no decent and respectable person would be caught dead or alive on Decatur Street." But for the ambitious, it was the place to be.

Harlem had Lenox Avenue, where the bourgeoisie and the near-to-do strolled. In Atlanta, there was Auburn Avenue, which was more sedate and focused than its counterpart, Decatur Street. Referred to as the "Negro Peachtree," Auburn Avenue was part residential and part business thoroughfare where African Americans began to migrate at the turn of the century. The street intersected the predominately white Peachtree Street, Atlanta's major business street, and linked the two races together, though the streets were as different as night as day. Anchored by Alonzo Herndon's Atlanta Life Insurance Company, Heman Perry's Citizens Trust Bank, and Yates and Milton Drug Store, small shops and stores were nestled in between. The businesses welcomed and hosted major conventions and conferences, including the National Business League in August of 1921. Over one thousand delegates attended and created economic vitality for the street. J.C. Ross was local president and Charles A. Shaw was secretary.

In 1924, insurance magnate Alonzo Franklin Herndon constructed a three-story office building at 251 Auburn, as well as a filling station adjacent to the building. The office building housed a number of black businesses, professional offices, and organizations, and contained one of the earliest hotel facilities catering to blacks. All of the African American's needs could be met on Auburn Avenue. People from the surrounding communities, such as Buttermilk Bottom and Old Fourth Ward, found along the street clothing stores, tailors, dress shops, markets, bakeries, offices of doctors, lawyers, and photographers, and dance halls, like the spacious Roof Garden Social Club. The William Business College was also located on the street. Every block on Auburn offered a religious institution. There were Big Bethel AME Church, (where Morris Brown College had been founded in 1881), Wheat Street Baptist Church, Ebenezer Baptist Church, and St. Mark AME Zion Church. What Decatur Street offered in crass, Auburn Avenue provided in class. It was on Auburn Avenue where the Atlanta Chapter of the NAACP was born in 1917. The chapter was the political catalyst for Black Atlanta during the decade of the twenties.

The Atlanta Chapter of the NAACP consisted of some of the most talented minds in city. James Weldon Johnson, a graduate of Atlanta University and the author of *Lift Ev'ry Voice and Sing,* who worked in the national office of the NAACP in New York, assisted businessmen Harry H. Pace and Truman Kelia Gibson, executives at the black-owned Standard Life Insurance Company, with the formation of the chapter. Johnson, then working as the field secretary for the organization, had also set up chapters in Athens, Augusta, Macon, and Savannah the same year.

The organizers of the Atlanta chapter delegation met at the home of Rev. Adam D. Williams, pastor of Ebenezer Baptist Church and grandfather of future civil rights leader Martin Luther King, Jr. Elected as its first officers were President Harry Pace and Secretary Walter White. By the end of March 1917, the chapter had 393 members, with 139 paid up memberships. James Weldon Johnson came back to Atlanta and heard Walter White speak to a full house at the Odd Fellow's Auditorium. Impressed with White's skills, Johnson invited him to come to New York City and work. White accepted the offer and resigned from the Atlanta Chapter. Pace also resigned as president and George Alexander Towns, a professor of pedagogy, was named president.

Two years later, in October of 1919, the office of the Southern Headquarters of the National Urban League was established by Jesse O. Thomas and a board was established consisting of Dr. John Hope, president of Morehouse College; Heman Perry; Solomon W. Walker, president of Pilgrim Life and Health Insurance; and many others. Lemuel L. Foster was named the first executive secretary, Cyrus Campfield was director of the Big Brother Movement, and Mae Maxwell was assistant industrial secretary. Together these two groups would confront and tackle the issues affecting African Americans in Atlanta during the 1920s. The League hosted and sponsored the Tri State Big Brother and Big Sister Conference, which brought together eighty delegates from three states to discuss the problems of underprivileged boys and girls.

The colleges continued to educate the masses with their academy, elementary, and high schools. ·Morehouse College created the Atlanta School of Social Work in 1920 and incorporated it 1924. Noted sociologist E. Franklin Frazier directed the program .

The Commission on Interracial Cooperation, or CIC, the most important interracial organization in Georgia and the South in the decade following World War I, was organized in Atlanta in 1919 by white liberals. The CIC was formed in the wake of the Atlanta Riot of 1906. By 1921, there were eight hundred local interracial councils throughout the South. Black participation in the CIC was never great, and declined after the first few years. The first black to join was John Hope, then president of Morehouse College. Hope joined when he returned from France in 1919. Mrs. Lugenia Burns Hope, wife of John Hope, helped to organize a group of African-American women as a part of a women's auxiliary. Efforts continued on all fronts to secure passage of an anti-lynching bill. The bill provided for fines against the county where lynching occurred and some of the fine money would be used to support dependents of the lynched. In 1921, *The New York World* estimated that as many as forty thousand Klansmen lived in Atlanta. Even though this was a severe overestimate, the sentiments of "Bring on you niggers!" echoed at Klan initiations at Stone Mountain and in Piedmont Park. Ironically, Booker T. Washington had given his speech "The Atlanta Compromise" at Piedmont Park in 1895.

By 1920, Atlanta's African-American population was 62,796, which represented 31% of the total population. The Atlanta Community Chest provided the civic arm for the less fortunate in the black community. Organizations such as the Carrie Steele Orphanage, Gate City Free Kindergarten, Leonard Street Orphanage, Neighborhood Union, the Phyllis Wheatley Branch of the YWCA, the Colored Department of the Associated Charities, the Anti Tuberculosis Association, the Travelers' Aid, and Georgia Committee on Race Relations worked to provide services for those in need.

The business community flourished. By the 1920s, there were seventy-two African-American businesses and twenty professional offices on Auburn Avenue, including the Butler Street YMCA, which opened in 1920 and became the meeting place for conventions that would come to town. The Herndon Office Building opened in 1924. The black-owned Atlanta State Savings Bank, established in 1909 to encourage blacks to save, failed in 1922, but paved the way for the Citizens Trust Company bank which was organized in 1921. The local chapter of the NAACP membership increased to three thousand by the end of 1920, under the presidency of the Rev. R.H. Singleton, who was pastor of Big Bethel AME Church until his death in 1923.

In 1920 in New York City, the National Convention of the Universal Negro Improvement Association (UNIA) met. Marcus Mosiah Garvey, "The Black Ponzi," spoke to approximately twenty-five thousand blacks during a rally at Madison Square Garden. A year later, he formally organized the Empire of Africa and appointed himself as the provisional president. He attempted to appeal, though unsuccessfully, to the League of Nations for permission to settle a colony in Africa. Garvey was ultimately convicted of mail fraud and sentenced to the federal penitentiary. He was transported to Atlanta in February of 1923, where he served a four-year sentence. He was released in November 1927 and was deported back to Jamaica.

Even though there were some Garvey supporters in Atlanta, most African Americans in the city were not interested in "going back to Africa." It was the era of "New Negro." By 1924–1929, African-American migration northward decreased, and the "New Negro" was considered less a threat to whites. Lynching declined, though there were isolated cases throughout Georgia.

Migration, urbanization, and military life, combined with the democratic rhetoric of the World War I, helped to intensify a new spirit of self-esteem among African Americans, along with the belief that their situation was intolerable. In the North, these forces led to the rise of both black nationalism and interracial cooperation, the Universal Negro Improvement Association, greater political activity, and the Harlem Renaissance. This period of great achievement for African Americans in art and literature featured writings from such persons as Countee Cullen, Claude McKay, Jean Toomer, James Weldon Johnson, Walter White, Georgia Douglass Johnson, Ama Bontemps, Langston Hughes, and Zora Neale Hurston. Hughes and Hurston were affectionately referred to as "Godfather" and "Godmother." Their work drew critical attention from both blacks and whites. Both Johnsons and White had Atlanta connections, both having attended Atlanta University. Toomer's classic book *Cane* was set in Georgia, where his distinguished grandfather P.B. S. Pinchback was born. In 1921, Toomer took a temporary job as superintendent of the Georgia Normal and Industrial Institute in Sparta, Georgia.

The book *The New Negro*, edited by Alaine Locke, created the foundation for the renaissance. The musical stage lit up in 1921 with Eubie Blake and Noble Sissle's *Shuffle Along*. (Atlanta would host the traveling stage review of this show in 1924.) The toast of Broadway was a little pixie-like dancer named Florence Mills, who wooed the hearts of all. In the chorus line of Florence's musical was a young dancer named Josephine Baker. Theatrical performances by Paul Robeson and Ethel Waters dominated the decade. The fervor of the spirit of the renaissance created a feeling of racial pride for African Americans, and the inability to express oneself creatively was removed at least temporarily.

The renaissance manifested itself in social, civic, and creative circles. Numerous literary, social and civic clubs, fraternities, and sororities were established in Atlanta. The decade of the twenties saw the flourishing of such established clubs as the Chatauqua Literary Circle, the Twelve Club, the Inquirers, the WGM'S, the Junior Matrons, and the Mo So Lit Club, which was founded in 1922. Some of the charter members of the latter were Mrs. W.J. Faulkner, Mrs. W.H. Cunningham, Mrs. J.E. Salter, Mrs. Lemuel L. Foster, Mrs. A.D. Hamilton, Mrs. J.O. Thomas, and others.

Arguably three of the most prestigious male groups were the Joymen Club, founded in 1912; the Kappa Boule of Sigma Pi Phi, chartered in 1920; and the 27 Club, founded in 1924. The 27 Club, which was organized by Dr. Edward G. Bowden, consisted of twenty-seven married men from ages twenty-seven to fifty, who met on the 27th day of each month at 7 minutes after 8. Men over fifty would be listed as Honorary members of the 27 Club.

Founded on January 24, 1920, Kappa Boule of Sigma Pi Phi's list of charter members reads like a who's who of Black Atlanta, including Samuel H. Archer, J.W.E. Bowen, Henry Rutherford Butler, C.C. Cater, L.C. Crogman, Truman K. Gibson, John Hope, Charles H. Johnson, William F. Penn, Thomas Heather Slater, George A. Towns, William J. Trent, and Austin T. Walden.

Most of the local graduate and undergraduate chapters of the eight Greek letter fraternities and sororities—Alpha Phi Alpha, Alpha Kappa Alpha, Delta Sigma Theta, Kappa Alpha Psi, Omega Psi Phi, Phi Beta Sigma, Sigma Gamma Rho, and Zeta Phi Beta—were established in Atlanta between 1919 and 1930, though several came much later. In 1921, both Phi Beta Sigma and Omega Psi Phi held their national conventions in Atlanta. They united in two resolutions calling for an inter-fraternal conference and supporting the Dyer Anti-Lynch bill.

These groups were very civic-minded, and while they enjoyed their annual dances and teas, reading and discussing the latest in literature, and competing in athletic competition, the issues confronting them had to be addressed.

Another group of organizations involved the Masonic lodges and their sister organizations, which included such groups as the Order of Calanthel, the Knights of Tabor, the Order of the Sphinx, the Daughters of Elks, and the Prince Hall affiliations—the largest in Georgia continued to provide outreach and pageantry to the community of Atlanta.

These developments from the new Negro in Atlanta contributed to changes in the city, where the new spirit posed a threat to white supremacy. This new spirit had hammered a few cracks in the caste system, despite frenzied counterattacks by the armies of its defenders, mobilized by the new Ku Klux Klan. The era of Jim Crow was still alive and well in Atlanta. The Atlanta City Council created "racial districts" within the city limits. Even so, black Atlantans found themselves still "in vogue" and were not to be left out of the decade of the Roaring Twenties and all that it had to offer. It was indeed a renaissance in Atlanta. The "voice" of Black Atlanta and the Republican and fraternal community was the *Atlanta Independent* newspaper, which was under the fiery editorship of Benjamin Davis, a staunch Republican. The paper helped to shape the thought of black Atlantans during the decade of the twenties, and featured strong writings from Jesse O. Thomas, Henry R. Butler, and Captain Jackson McHenry, as well as editorial cartoons from P.S. Cooke. It ceased publication in 1928, and the *Atlanta World,* published by the Scott family, began the same year. The paper featured columnist I.P. Reynolds, whose column "Sam of Auburn Avenue" chronicled the happenings of the street.

As the decade closed, many of the African-American community luminaries passed on, creating a void in leadership and wealth. Three of the most notables included Internal Revenue Collector Henry Rucker in 1924, banker Heman Perry, boxer Theodore "Tiger" Flowers, and insurance magnate Alonzo Franklin Herndon, both of whom died in 1927. On January 15, 1929, in a house on Auburn Avenue, Michael Luther King (later to change his name to Martin) was born to M.L. and Alberta Williams King. The stock market crashed in October of 1929 and forced many businesses to regroup, but the African-American community, in areas social, civic, educational and political, all remained "in vogue."

Claude McKay   Countee Cullen

One

"The New Negro in Atlanta"

"Up you mighty race! You can accomplish what you will!"
Marcus Garvey

Pictured here are the founders of the Atlanta chapter of the NAACP, organized in 1917. From left to right are: (seated) Harry Pace, Dr. Charles Johnson, Dr. Louis T. Wright, and Walter F. White; (standing) Peyton Allen, George Towns, Benjamin Davis, Rev. L.H. King, Dr. William F. Penn, Dr. John Hope, and David H. Sims. Walter White was born in Atlanta in 1893 to middle-class parents. His mother was one-sixteenth black, and his father, who was one-quarter black, worked for the post office. White worked for Standard Life Insurance Company. He wrote two novels, *The Fire in the Flint,* in 1924, and *Flint,* in 1926, which dealt with lynching and passing. He joined the NAACP as a full-time executive in 1919. (Library of Congress.)

African-American soldiers from Camp Gordon in DeKalb County and auxiliary groups poured into the streets of Atlanta in a gallant parade the day after the Germans signed an armistice. Camp Gordon was one of the largest training centers for Negro troops, housing over nine thousand blacks by 1917. Most of the black recruits were assigned to engineer or labor service battalions. The end of the war was a major relief for the troops segregated in their service for their country. Mayor Candler called for a victory parade on November 12, 1918, and the troops marched down Peachtree Street near 10th Street to Whitehall Street as these two photos show. (Digging It Up Archives.)

The CRISIS

Vol. 17—No. 4   FEBRUARY, 1919   Whole No. 100

The cover of the *Crisis* for February 1919 featured Atlantan Austin T. Walden, a 1907 graduate of Atlanta University. He also finished the University of Michigan Law School in 1911. Walden had a stellar career in law as one of three African-American men admitted to the Georgia Bar to practice law in Atlanta during the 1920s. Walden served in the 365th Infantry, and was an active member of the Republican Party. He practiced on Auburn Avenue before acquiring his own building on Butler Street. Walden was born in Fort Valley, Georgia.

Jesse O. Thomas helped to establish the Atlanta chapter of the National Urban League in 1919 and served as secretary. He was a member of Omega Psi Phi Fraternity, and wrote for the *Atlanta Independent* newspaper. After fire destroyed Big Bethel Church in 1923, Thomas, though not a member, volunteered his services to raise money to rebuild the church, raising over $10,000. (Digging It Up Archives.)

By 1920, Atlanta's population was growing, and so was the construction of buildings. Whitehall Street shows the hustle and bustle of life in Atlanta in the 1920s.

Shown here is the intersection of Peachtree and Forsyth Streets. To the right is the Lyric Theater, and in the bottom right-hand corner is the Lowe's Grand Theater, both of which had Jim Crow rules for African Americans, who were forced to sit in the balcony. (Digging It Up Archives.)

Delivery boys pose beside their motorcycles in front of Munn's Drugstore on Broad Street, c. 1920. (Atlanta History Center.)

One of several Herndon's Bath and Barber shops was nestled near the Metropolitan Theater on N. Broad Street. Alonzo Herndon represented the hopes and dreams of African Americans seeking economic prosperity. A former slave, by 1920 Herndon had amassed a sizable amount of property throughout the city and had partnered in numerous business ventures, including Southview Cemetery, Atlanta State Savings Bank, and Standard Life Insurance Company. During the 1920s, he would construct an office building and filling station on Auburn Avenue, a street often described as "The Negro Peachtree." (The Herndon Foundation.)

In 1920, Atlanta Mutual Insurance Company and Alonzo Herndon occupied and renovated a residence and purchased an additional lot at 132 Auburn in the same block. The upper level was rented out to other businesses and organizations, including one of the first offices of photographer Paul Poole. (The Herndon Foundation.)

Two

Auburn Avenue

"The Negro Was in Vogue"
Langston Hughes

By 1920, Auburn Avenue had become the commercial hub of Black Atlanta. Known as Wheat Street until 1893, this street was the heart and soul of African-American life, providing the center for business, social, cultural, and religious life for black Atlantans. It was close to the central business district, and adjacent to the residential area for leading African Americans. The commercial district contained the city's leading black enterprises and institutions: real estate and construction firms, newspapers and funeral homes, insurance companies and banks. All along "the avenue" from Courtland Street to Jackson Street were the offices of African-American physicians, dentists, craftsmen, carpenters, and plumbers and the smaller businesses such as floral shops, groceries, dry cleaners, restaurants, and photography studios. Churches, fraternal orders, hotels, and entertainment establishments contributed to the vitality of the area and characterized the self-help philosophy that permeated the avenue. (Digging It Up Archives.)

The Odd Fellow Auditorium and Office Building was constructed in 1912 and 1914, respectively, under the leadership of Benjamin Davis and the Grand Order of Odd Fellows. The building included office space, the Atlanta State Savings Bank, and featured the Roof Garden, a dance hall under the auspices of the Fulton Social Club and operated by Bill Shaw, who was also business manager of the *Atlanta Independent*. By the 1920s, the Paramount Theater provided movies featuring a pipe organ and seating for over one thousand. Published from the fifth floor was the *Atlanta Independent*. Davis served as editor, B.F. Cofer was managing editor, and Miss Ola M. Walker was business manager. Yearly subscription price was $1.50. In 1923, Heman Perry purchased the building, later passing it to the National Benefit Life Insurance Company. (Digging It Up Archives.)

The Atlanta Mutual Insurance Company Leadership Club stands in front of the entrance of the Odd Fellow Building. Alonzo Herndon, the former slave and barber, founded the Insurance Company in 1905. By mid-1925, the company had over $600,000 in assets and operated in eight states. Other officers were R.W. Chamblee, E.M. Martin, and Lemuel Haywood. Alonzo Herndon served as president of the company until his death in 1927. (The Herndon Foundation.)

On the corner of Auburn Avenue and Butler Street was the Gate City Drug Store, founded by Moses Amos, who is standing in front of the store. Moses was born in 1866 in rural Georgia. In 1876, at the age of ten, Moses walked to Atlanta and found a job working with Dr. J.C. Huss, a white physician who operated a pharmacy in a two-story white house on this corner. In 1912, the District Grand Lodge of the Odd Fellows purchased this corner lot. Later, Dr. Thomas Heathe Slater and Dr. Henry Butler sold their interest to Moses Amos. The old store was torn down, and on June 10, 1914, Amos re-opened the store. He was also awarded his pharmacy license the same year, becoming the first African-American pharmacist in the state of Georgia. Doctor Amos operated this store until 1922, when he relocated to the West Side. He died in 1929. (Digging It Up Archives.)

There were numerous other stores, shops, sundries, and restaurants on Auburn during the 1920s, including Ma Suttons, the Red Rock Bottling Company, and Blocker's Groceries. This advertisement is from the James E. Jordan's Department Store on the corner of Auburn Avenue and Butler Street, c. 1927.

OUR NEW HOME
and **PERSONNEL**
Now Located in Our
NEW STORE
CARRYING A FULL AND COMPLETE LINE OF
Clothing
Furnishings
Hats, Caps
AND
Ladies' Ready to-Wear
IVY 8363

J. E. JORDAN
President and Manager

MRS. M. L. GLENN
Manager Ladies' Wear Department

R. L. HAYNES
Manager Tailoring Department

C. C. SHANKS
Auditor

Corner
Auburn Ave.
and Butler

JORDAN'S

Corner
Auburn Ave.
and Butler

Heman Perry (middle), Harry Pace (left), and Alonzo Franklin Herndon (right) were three of the most phenomenal businessmen in Atlanta. Perry, a native of Houston, Texas, arrived in Atlanta in 1908 and established a number of businesses including Standard Life Insurance Company, the first legal reserve company among blacks, as well as the Service Companies, which included a realty, construction, printing, and laundry division. Pace was born in Covington, Georgia, in 1884. He was secretary-treasurer of Standard Life and owned the Black Star Record Company. In 1929, he acquired the Supreme Liberty Life Insurance Company in Chicago. (Digging It Up Archives.)

In 1921, Perry opened the Citizens Trust Bank on Auburn Avenue in an old fish market on the bottom floor of the building. Entities of Perry's such as the Service Company, Service Realty Service Engineer and Construction Company, and Standard Life were housed in the building in 1923. The top floor had a right side entrance that led to the McKay Hotel, later to be renamed the Royal Hotel. The left side of the building had an entrance which led to the offices of the *Atlanta Daily World* newspaper. The opening of this bank, along with other large withdrawals which undermined the bank, led to the closing of the Atlanta State Savings Bank in the Odd Fellow building on February 15, 1922. (Digging It Up Archives.)

In this photograph, Norris Herndon, a graduate of Atlanta University, is standing in front of his car near the garage at his home on University Place. The only son of Alonzo and Adrienne Herndon, Norris returned to Atlanta and joined Atlanta Life after graduating from Harvard University, where he received his Master's Degree in Business Administration in 1921. While at Harvard, Norris pledged the Sigma Chapter of Alpha Phi Alpha. When he returned, he joined Atlanta Life as vice-president and cashier. In 1928, he was elected the company's second president, and he began a program of expansion to other states, including Texas, Florida, Kentucky, and Ohio. (The Herndon Foundation.)

The Auburn Branch of the Carnegie Library, located on the corner of Auburn and Fort Street, had a rich history. Dr. W.E.B. DuBois had appeared before the library board when the white branch opened, demanding full rights for blacks to use the building, but was denied. It later took a concerted effort between city government and the black leadership of Atlanta to erect this branch. Mayor Key, who had served from 1919 to 1922, had drawn the support of the black community with his actions, including vetoing a Klan-sponsored motion condemning the Knights of Columbus and prohibiting masked parades on city streets. He also helped African Americans to obtain a park and swimming pool on the West Side of Atlanta.

With a generous donation from Andrew Carnegie, the Auburn Branch Library opened. Key's support of African Americans, as well as other causes, resulted in his defeat in 1922 and 1924 to Klansman Walter A. Sims. On one occasion, Sims had even referred to Key on the rostrum as "nigger lover." (Annie McPheeters.)

21

The first librarian at the Auburn branch was Alice Dugged Cary, a native of Michigan and a pioneer in education, who, along with DuBois and others, worked feverishly to get the "colored" branch opened. She was the second principal of Morris Brown University in 1885 and the first principal of Mitchell Street School; she had an illustrious career as an educator before going into library service. "Mother Cary," as she was known, helped to establish the second chapter of Zeta Phi Beta Sorority in 1921, and was a honorary member of the Utopian Literary Club. (Annie McPheeters.)

During World War I, the Cox brothers had invested substantially in Liberty Bonds to show their patriotism. By 1920, Cox Brothers Funeral Home was celebrating its second decade, having been established in 1900. Mr. Charles Cox is standing in front of the Cox Funeral Home, next to a new funeral hearse built by Michigan Hearse and Motor Company out of Grand Rapids, Michigan. The building was erected in 1923 by Heman's Perry Service Construction Company. There was also a branch office in East Point. Cox married Addie Turner in 1930, and they operated and resided in this building until 1935. (Digging It Up Archives.)

Standing on the steps of the Atlanta Mutual Building, c. 1921, are the founding members and brothers of the Atlanta chapter of Alpha Phi Alpha Fraternity. The chapter was founded on May 20, 1920. The group held its meetings in the building owned by Alonzo Franklin Herndon, a member of the chapter and founder of the insurance company.
Also, located in the building were the General Missionary Baptist Convention and Paul Poole's studio. (Digging It Up Archives.)

Alex Harvey opened the Silver Moon barbershop on the corner of Auburn Avenue and Butler Street in 1904. By the 1920s, it was one of the oldest and continuous businesses on the street. (Claudine Blake/Digging It Up Archives.)

In 1920, as a response from Governor Hugh Dorsey of Georgia, the NAACP held its annual conference at Big Bethel AME Church. It was the first time that the organization's meeting had been held in the South. In attendance were W.E.B. DuBois, James Weldon Johnson, and Atlanta native Walter White, a major figure in New York and the Harlem Renaissance. The issue of race relations was one of the major topics. DuBois said "We go to Atlanta to say to the South that we want to vote, stop lynching, improve schools, end Jim Crow and peonage, and obtain decent wages and treatment." (Reprinted from *The Crisis.*)

Moses Amos sold the Gate City Drug Store to the Heman Perry Enterprises, and it was known for a short time as the Service Pharmacy. Two businessmen, Clayton R. Yates and Lorimer D. Milton, formed a partnership in April of 1924 and acquired the store and renamed it Yates and Milton Drug Store. The two later established a chain of drugstores. There were over five stores throughout Atlanta. (Digging It Up Archives.)

Clayton Russell Yates , a native of
Springfield, Ohio, came to Atlanta to
attend Atlanta University after
studying at Tuskegee University.
Yates graduated in 1920, and began
work as a teller and later assistant
cashier of the Citizens Trust Company
before being elected chairman of the
board of directors of the Citizens Trust
Company. In 1925, Yates, Milton, and
Blayton acquired the Citizens Trust
bank. Yates was also a founder of the
Atlanta Negro Voters League.
(*Atlanta Daily World.*)

Lorimer Douglas Milton, a native of Prince
William, Virginia, graduated from Brown
University in 1920. He moved to Atlanta in 1921,
when he was hired by Morehouse College
President John Hope to teach at Morehouse. He
was elected as secretary in 1923, cashier and
treasurer of Citizens Trust in 1927, and in 1930,
was elected president of the bank. He also served
at Atlanta University as professor in the School of
Business Administration, which he and J.B.
Blayton, his business partner, helped to establish.
(*Atlanta Daily World.*)

The Curry and Hall Style Shop for men was opened by Oscar Hall (right) and T.J. Curry (left) in 1920 on Auburn Avenue. The shop sold hats and men's accessories and was a very popular store. In 1928, Hall and Leroy Carter opened a filling station on the same street. (Digging It Up Archives.)

In 1929, William (left) and Albert C. Murdaugh opened their funeral home on the corner of Auburn and Piedmont Avenues. A few years later they acquired the David T. Howard Funeral Home and merged the two. (Digging It Up Archives.)

John Wesley Dobbs came to Atlanta from Kennesaw, Georgia. He graduated from the Atlanta Baptist Academy, and worked at a drugstore on Houston and Piedmont. In 1903, he began his career as a railway mail clerk for the Nashville and Atlanta Railway Postal Office. He married Irene Thompson, from Columbus, Mississippi, in 1906. By the 1920s, the Dobbs were the parents of six daughters and resided at 540 Houston Street. Dobbs sold insurance for the Standard Realty Insurance Company during the 1920s. He was elected secretary of the Prince Hall Grand Masonic Lodge in 1924 and had an office in the Odd Fellows Building on Auburn Avenue. He was elected grand master of the lodge in 1932. (Andre Vann/Josephine Dobbs Clements.)

In 1924, Alonzo Herndon demolished the Chandler Brothers Undertakers and Butler's Restaurant at the corner of Auburn and Butler Street and constructed a building which contained a branch office of Atlanta Life, the Maise Department Store, and James Jordan's Tailoring Shop. The upper levels would later be occupied by the Apex Beauty School, the Atlanta University School of Social Work (1925–1933), and Blayton's School of Accounting. The Savoy Hotel opened in 1930. The structure was next to the newly constructed three-story office building also constructed by Herndon. (The Herndon Foundation.)

On October 31, 1925, fifteen men invested $100 each to start Mutual Federal Savings and Loan Company. Pictured here are three of the founders: J. Garland Woods (top left); Joseph H.B. Evans (top right); and Jesse B. Blayton (bottom). The other founders not pictured are: C.C. Hart (the first licensed black plumber in Atlanta), Thomas J. Henry (attorney), Henry M. Ivey (funeral director), A.M. Carter, W.P. Adams, Charles E. Arnold, T.J. Ferguson (Standard Life Insurance executive), Dr. Charles Johnson, David Dallas Jones, and Dr. Thomas Heathe Slater. Henry Ivey and Dr. Slater are pictured in other parts of the book. (Digging It Up Archives.)

Just around the corner from the Odd Fellows Building on Bell Street, Jesse Hanley, a mortician, acquired the old Independent Benevolent Protective Order building in 1929 and relocated his funeral home from Edgewood Avenue, where it had been since 1921. The building had been constructed in 1915 by William S. Cannon, and also housed the Reginall Laboratory, which had been founded by W.S. Cannon. Mr. Hanley had one of the largest fleet of cars and hearses. Here the staff at Hanley's stand in front of his lead car, which once belonged to boxer Tiger Flowers. It was given to Mr. Hanley after Tiger's death in 1927. (Digging It Up Archives.)

William S. Cannon was president and founder of the Reginall Laboratory. His hair preparation company manufactured Cocoa Balm, Skin Food and Whitener, Shampoo and Jelly, Pressing Oil, and Toilet Soap costing 25¢ and 35¢. Cannon later sold his building to Hanley in 1929 and moved to Ashby Street. This company was the predecessor to the Cannonlene Hair Company and School located on Hunter Street in the 1930s. (Digging It Up Archives.)

Hostesses for the National Negro Insurance Association meeting in Atlanta pose for this picture in front of the Atlanta Life Building, *c*. 1920.

These photographs were taken at the Mondul Studio in the Odd Fellows Auditorium building on Auburn Avenue. Mondul was a native of East India who had come to Atlanta and added his ethnic background to the business community on Auburn Avenue. He was the most successful African-American photographer in Atlanta until 1927. Later, Paul Poole would establish himself as "the" photographer of Black Atlanta during the Roaring Twenties. (Digging It Up Archives.)

Three
Paul Poole

Black Harlem in New York had James Vanderzee photographing the beauty of its renaissance, and Black Atlanta had Paul Poole to capture its essence, especially during the 1920s. Born in Sandersville, Georgia, in 1886 to Samuel Poole, a shoemaker, and Cora Poole, Paul Poole lived along with his family in the old Fourth Ward area on Ezzard Street. By 1911, Poole was employed as a photo finisher for photographer C.F. McDonnell. In 1920, McDonnell's studio was sold to a commercial photographer. Poole branched out on his own and opened a studio in the Atlanta Mutual Insurance Company Building at 132 Auburn Avenue. Poole enjoyed great recognition as the revered photographer of Black Atlanta in the decades of the 1920s and 1930s until another photographer, Andrew T. Kelly, emerged. Poole is believed to have moved to Chicago. (Digging It Up Archives.)

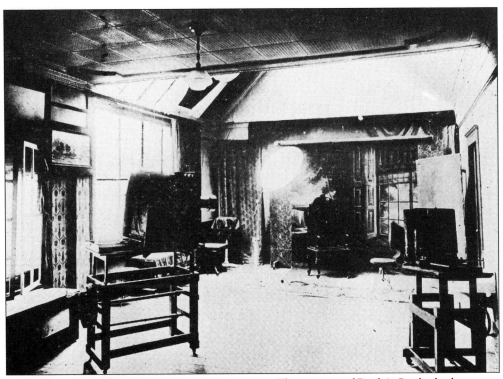

The interior of Poole's Studio had many different backdrops used for settings. Poole also had a picture window where displays of his photographic works were seen. His very elegant and artistic photographs used soft lighting and were printed in sepia. (*The Aurora*, Morris Brown Yearbook, 1923.)

Poole photographed India Delaine Amos, the wife of Miles Amos. She graduated from Fisk University in 1930 and was part owner and manager of Amos Drug Store. She was a member of the WGM and the Chautauqua Circle, *c.* 1920. (Emma Amos.)

Nellie Askew, the fashionable and stylish daughter of Thomas and Mary Askew, is pictured here, *c.* 1920, in a photo by Poole. (Isaiah Sloan Blocker.)

Four generations of the Askew family are pictured here in this *c.* 1921 photograph. From left to right are: Minnie Askew Davis, Mary W. Askew (seated), Isaiah Sloan Blocker (grandson), and Georgia Davis Blocker. Thomas Askew, husband of Mary, was Atlanta's first African-American photographer. Born in the 1850s, Thomas began his photography in the 1880s at Motes Studio in downtown Atlanta. The Askews and their nine children resided at 114 Summit Avenue and were burned out during Atlanta's great fire of 1917.(Isaiah Sloan Blocker.)

Left: This unidentified young girl's dress characterizes the styles of the 1920s. (Digging It Up Archives.)

Right: Shown here is Clara Lenore Yates, daughter of Clayton and Mae Yates. Clara attended the Oglethorpe School, Atlanta University Laboratory High, and Spelman College, *c.* 1931. (Clara Yates.)

Poole's portraits of children were most delightful. On the left is an image of two unidentified young girls, *c.* 1924, and on the right is a photograph of baby Vernon Buck, *c.* 1920. (Digging It Up Archives.)

34

Left: Mrs. Ann B. Cooper and daughter are pictured here, *c.* 1923. She was the wife of Auburn Avenue dentist Dr. A.B. Cooper. (Ann B. Cooper.)

Right: Mrs. Josephine Dibble Murphy, pictured here with with baby son Harry, was the wife of Auburn Avenue printer and journalist Harry S. Murphy. (Harry S. Murphy.)

Left: Here, the Wardlaw twins, Albert and Alvin, pose in sailor suits for Mr. Poole, *c.* 1927. (Albert Wardlaw.)

Right: The unidentified young man in this *c.* 1924 photograph was a student at one of the Atlanta University Center schools. Just below his vest is his Alpha Phi Alpha Fraternity badge. (Willis Jones/Digging It Up Archives.)

The unidentified church group in this c. 1922 photograph has obviously lost a member of the group, as the empty chair and flower symbolizes the lost member. (Digging It Up Archives.)

Elizabeth Landrum and her bridesmaid and nieces Ethyl (far right) and Jeanette Harvey (far left), daughters of Elizabeth's sister Mae and B.T. Harvey, posed for Mr. Poole, c. 1923. Both girls, Ethyl and Jeanette, would go on to Morris Brown College, where they chartered the school's chapter of Alpha Kappa Alpha Sorority in 1942. (Jeanette Harvey Hamme.)

The wedding of Eugene M. Martin to Helen White was one of the social events of the season in 1926. Pictured from left to right are: (front row) flower girl Yvonne Braithwaite, Eugene M. Martin, Helen White, George White (father of the bride), and ring bearer Walter D. Westmoreland; (back row) Rev. William Faulkner, Hazel Rucker, Norris Herndon, Madeline White, Walter Aiken, unidentified, unidentified, Grace Nash, and Walter Smith. (Atlanta History Center.)

This dapperly dressed man in his three-piece striped suit and bow tie was photographed by Mr. Poole, c. 1924. (Edward Bowen.)

Miles Amos was the nephew of Dr. Moses Amos. In 1923, they opened Amos Drug Store on the corner of Hunter and Ashby Streets, where Miles ran the store until it closed in 1969. He graduated from Wilberforce University and had planned to study law, but entered the Cincinnati College of Pharmacy, where he graduated in 1923. (Emma Amos.)

Mr. Poole photographed the distinguished pastor of the First Congregational Church, Rev. Russell Brown. Rev. Brown was pastor of the church from the 1910s to 1924, when he relocated to Cleveland, Ohio. (Digging It Up Archives.)

Here, Mrs. Pattie Holmes, wife of Dr. Hamilton Holmes and one of the founders of the National Association of Colored Graduate Nurses, poses with her children. Pictured, from left to right, are Hamilton, Oliver, Mrs. Holmes, Alice Dugged, and Alfred. (Alice Holmes Washington.)

Here, Rev. William Faulkner, pastor of the First Congregational Church, is surrounded by his wife, Bess, and their children: William, known as Billy, and Josephine (seated in Rev. Faulkner's lap). Mrs. Faulkner was a founder of the Mo So Lit Club, which was established in 1922. Rev. Faulkner served as Basileus of Omega Psi Phi Fraternity, and was also a partner with Walter Aiken in the Aiken and Faulkner Real Estate Building, Loan and Construction Company on Auburn Avenue. (Atlanta History Center.)

Pictured here, from left to right, is the Harper family: Mae Earline, Carrie Bell Nichols Harper, Charles Lincoln Harper, and William Nicholas Harper. Professor C.L. Harper was born in 1877 in Sparta, Georgia. He was a graduate of Morris Brown College and became the first principal of the High School Department; he was also the principal of the Yonge Street Night School from 1915 to 1924. In 1924, he was appointed as the first principal of the Booker T. Washington High School, and served there for eighteen years. Harper was also president of the Atlanta chapter of the NAACP. Mrs. Harper held memberships in numerous clubs, including the Utopian Literary Club. This family portrait was taken by Poole. (Atlanta History Center.)

These five friends, whose families were pioneer Atlantans, celebrated their graduation from Atlanta University in 1924. Pictured are: (clockwise, far left) Mildred Greenwood, Eloise Murphy, Madeline White, Nell Hamilton, and Helen White. Mildred Greenwood married musician and composer Frederick Douglas Hall. Eloise Murphy, granddaughter of David T. Howard, married banker Lorimer Milton. Helen White and Madeline White were sisters of NAACP executive Walter White. Nell Hamilton was the daughter of pioneer builder Alexander D. Hamilton. (Rose Palmer.)

The older Wardlaw children posed for this photograph, c. 1920 From left to right are: (seated) Lydia and Mildred; (standing) James Tapley and Charles Hamilton Wardlaw. The children resided with their parents on Fair Street. (Albert Wardlaw.)

Here, Mrs. Emmeline Southhall Scott, from Mississippi, is surrounded by her sons. From left to right, they are Emel, Aurelius, Lewis, W.A. Scott, Cornelius Scott, and Lewis. William A. Scott founded the *Atlanta World* on August 5, 1928. It was the second newspaper to be published in the city after the *Independent* ceased operation in 1928. The *World* was founded as a weekly, and became a semi-weekly in May of 1930, a tri-weekly on April 20, 1931, and a daily (except Monday) in March of 1932. The *World* was a part of the Scott Newspaper Syndicate, which was comprised of weeklies and semi-weeklies in Memphis; Columbus, Georgia; Birmingham; and other Southeastern cities. W.A. Scott was killed in February of 1934, and his brother C.A. Scott succeeded him as editor and general manager of the paper. (Ruth Scott Simmons.)

The Atlanta Black Crackers Baseball team was organized in 1919. By 1920, it was under the ownership of Bill Shaw and consisted of very talented players. Shaw was a most industrious businessman, operating a restaurant, running the Roof Garden, and ultimately purchasing the Odd Fellows Building in 1935. He later sold the building to the Georgia Baptist Convention. The Black Crackers were members of the Southern Colored League teams, and the games were played at the Morris Brown University field and the old Spiller's Field across from what would become the Ponce De Leon Ballpark. (Edward Bowen.)

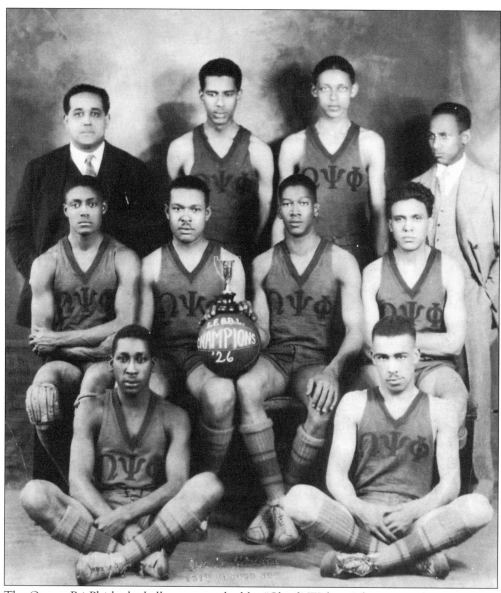

The Omega Psi Phi basketball team, coached by "Chief" Walter Aiken, were the 1926 inter-fraternity basketball champions. The team consisted of members from Tau Chapter at Atlanta University, Psi Chapter at Morehouse, and Beta Psi Chapter at Clark College. The fraternity was established in Atlanta on December 27, 1919, as the Eta Omega Chapter, and was composed of college men from Morehouse, Clark, and Atlanta University during the 1920s. Harold H. Thomas, Harvey Smith, L.R. Harper, Horace A. Hodges, and C.E. Warner organized the chapter. In 1924, they opened a fraternity house on Ashby Street. Some prominent Omega men during the 1920s were W.J. Faulkner, Jesse O. Thomas, C.L. Harper, and John Wesley Dobbs. This team portrait was taken by Paul Poole. (Digging It Up Archives.)

Big Tournament and Prom!!
Come! See the Four Fraternities Engage in the most Thrilling

Basket Ball Games

OF THE SEASON

At last the Public has what it has been longing for--a thrilling Inter-Fraternity Tournament deciding the "Inter-frat Champs" followed by the Season's Biggest Hit

A Real Inter-Fraternity Dance

TAFT HALL

AUDITORIUM-ARMORY

SATURDAY
MARCH 6, 1926

Game: 8 P. M.   Dance: 10 P. M.

ADMISSION 35c   COUPLE 50c
GOOD MUSIC
REFRESHMENTS

The Inter-Fraternity Basketball Council was established in 1925 at the Butler Street YMCA. Cornelius V. Troup, a member of Phi Beta Sigma, served as president. The games were played at Taft Hall at the City Auditorium, as this 1926 flyer shows. (Digging It Up Archives.)

Nish Williams (left), a resident of the Fourth Ward, attended and played baseball for Morehouse College during the early 1920s. Nish later moved to the Negro League, playing with the Nashville and Baltimore Elite Giants. He returned to Atlanta with his wife to open a restaurant, William's Tavern, in the 1940s on Hunter Street. (Edward Bowen.)

Four

The West Side Story

With the mass movement of African-American families from the Old Fourth Ward to the West Side of Atlanta following the Fire of 1917, Heman Perry's development of moderate middle-class housing, known as Ashby Heights and Washington Park, and the construction of Booker T. Washington High School in 1923, the West Side of Atlanta flourished. On May 19, 1919, a contest to name the new community resulted in the name Ashby Heights being selected. As a result, numerous businesses opened on Ashby and Hunter Streets, including the No Brake School of Hair Dressing, W.J. Rhodes Filling Station, and Amos Drug Store in 1923. The drugstore was a landmark in the community, and operated until 1969. In this picture, an unidentified man stands next to a car in a driveway of one of the numerous residences on Hunter Street in the West Side. (Emma Amos.)

A.W. Parks opened the Parks Shoe Rebuilders at 854 Hunter Street in 1922. The Parks family resided on Ashby Grove. Also living in the area was Lena Horne. Horne moved to Atlanta from Fort Valley, Georgia, and resided on Hunter Street (what is now the *Atlanta Inquirer Office*) and attended Booker T. Washington High School. Her home was in the heart of the West Side Community, within walking distance from Booker T. Washington High School and few houses from the Ashby Theater. She moved to Brooklyn in 1929. (Digging It Up Archives.)

Mabel Driskell (*c.* 1923) and her husband, William (not shown), founded the Dermis Cura School of Hair and Beauty Culture around 1913. Mrs. Driskell graduated with the first class of nurses from Morris Brown in 1905. Mr. Driskell was a former Standard Life Insurance Company employee. The school was located in a two-story building at 479 Tattnall Street, near Northside Drive (between Beckwith and Chapel Streets). The school had a small dormitory upstairs, trained students in Atlanta and throughout the country, and made hair preparations on-site. Some of the products the Driskells prepared included Invigorating Oil, which was tar-based, and liquid hair grower and shampoos. There were also large vats where Mrs. Driskell mixed her chemicals.

Mrs. Bessie Walker McElroy operated the La France Tea Room on Hunter Street during the 1920s. Her sister, Mary Walker James, and her husband operated the James Hotel on Auburn Avenue and opened the James Cafe on Hunter Street. (Walter "Billy" Reid.)

Charles Cater, a former mail carrier, was a well-respected businessman. He owned several stores, including the grocery store on the corner of Mayson Turner and Hunter Streets during the 1920s. Cater served on the board of the Fair Haven Hospital, was a charter member of Kappa Boule of Sigma Pi Phi Fraternity, and served as cashier for the Atlanta State Savings Bank and Standard Life Insurance Company. Cater had previously operated a store in the old Fourth Ward community. He and his first wife, Mary Tate, had several children: C.C. Jr., a physician; Douglas and Roscoe, managers of the grocery stores; and Hattie, an educator at Talladega.

In 1927, J.H. Sellers and Samuel Garrett Sellers established the Seller Brothers Funeral Home on Hunter Street. In this c. 1931 photograph, they are shown loading up three hearses in the center of Hunter Street. The funeral home is now under the leadership of Juanita Sellers Stone, the daughter of Samuel Sellers. (Juanita Sellers Stone.)

Arthur H. Yancey, born in the Darktown area of Cummings, Georgia, was a carrier for the U.S. Post Office. In 1912, he built this very nice home for his wife, the former Daisy L. Sherard, and their seven children on Beckwith Street, near the Atlanta University Campus and next to the Knowles Industrial Building. (Asa Yancey.)

Five
Church and Religion

A women's auxiliary group of the Grant Chapel AME Church in East Point, Georgia, pose outside of the church in this *c.* 1922 photograph. There were hundreds of churches throughout Atlanta, covering all denominations, including the Bishop King H. Burris Bethlehem Church of God movement, which acquired the Crystal Theater on Hunter Street for its church. On Boulevard, the first Catholic church for blacks had been established in 1911. After eight years of meeting in a storefront on Edgewood Avenue, Ebenezer Baptist Church moved to Auburn Avenue in 1922 under the leadership of Rev. A.D. Williams. His son-in-law, Rev. Martin Luther King Sr. became assistant pastor in 1927. King was later to succeed Williams as pastor. (Alice Washington.)

Rev. Peter James Bryant was a major leader in the African-American community. He became pastor of Wheat Street in 1898, organized the Atlanta Benevolent Protective Association in 1904, and was associate editor of the *Voice of the Negro*, a monthly magazine. He was also chairman of the board of the Carrie Steele orphanage. His wife, Sylvia Bryant, operated the Bryant Baptist Institute on Auburn Avenue and was the first president of the Phyllis Wheatley YWCA. Rev. Bryant and his wife were pillars in the civic and religious life in Atlanta. In 1920, Rev. Bryant and his congregation moved into a new sanctuary on the corner of Auburn and Hilliard Street. The Gothic Revival structure was built by African-American contractor Robert E. Pharrow, who also built the Odd Fellows Building. (Digging It Up Archives.)

Rev. Leander A. Pinkston was one of the talented and gifted young Baptist ministers in Atlanta during the 1920s. He was pastor at one of two churches called Beulah Baptist. This church was located on the corner of Hunnicutt and Williams Street. (Digging It Up Archives.)

Two years after the completion of extended renovation work on Big Bethel AME Church and the addition of the lighted cross on the steeple, bearing the message "Jesus Saves," a devastating fire broke out on February 17, 1923, at 2:30 pm. The fire was discovered by a passerby, and two fire stations responded. The fire spread throughout the building, and the roof and tower caved in, causing a portion of the interior wall to collapse. Only the exterior walls and the facade of the new Moller Pipe Organ stood. The cause of the fire was not determined and damage totaled $250,000. The church's insurance had expired the day before the fire. Rev. R.H. Singleton was pastor at the time. (Digging It Up Archives.)

Allen Temple AME Church was located in Summerhill, on the corner of Fraser and Clarke Streets. (Georgia State Archives.)

Entering the decade of the 1920s, the dean of African-American ministers was Rev. Edward Randolph Carter, pastor of Friendship Baptist Church for over forty years. Rev. Carter, a Morehouse College graduate and member of the Morehouse College Board of Trustees, resided on Tatnall Street with his wife, Obelia Cecile, and their children: Edward Jr., a pharmacist; Raymond H. Carter, a physician; James, a U.S. Post Office specialist; Iola, an artist; and Earnest, a Pullman porter. Rev. Carter operated the Carter Home for the elderly on Haynes and West Mitchell Street. (Digging It Up Archives.)

In 1923, the Second Seventh Day Adventist Church was constructed on Ashby Street on the Westside of Atlanta. The inset is of Elder F.H. Savage. (Digging It Up Archives.)

This unidentified couple stands in front of the West Mitchell CME Church on W. Mitchell Street near Tatnall and the Atlanta University campus, c. 1920. Other CME churches in Atlanta were Butler Street and Holsey Temple. (Digging It Up Archives.)

W.B. Loving Clark was pastor of Allen Temple AME Church on Fraser Street in the Summerhill community. Rev. Clark was a delegate to the General Conference in 1928, secretary of the Episcopal Committee, and member of the Church Extension Board. (Digging It Up Archives.)

By 1920, Warren Memorial Methodist Church had been at this location on the corner of Greensferry Avenue and Mildred Street for six years, having been moved in 1914, by Rev. Elijah Henry Oliver, who died in 1920. The church was partially destroyed by fire in December 1929, during the pastorate of Rev. S.M. Miller. (Digging It Up Archives.)

Six

Education and Politics

The struggle to obtain equal education for African-American students in Atlanta had reached a pinnacle by 1920. The quest had become a "crisis" for all those involved and affected by the disparity in conditions, resources, and teacher pay. There were fifteen schools for "colored" children in Atlanta by December 1921. They included Ashby Street, South Atlanta, Gray Street, Yonge Street, Roach Street, Mitchell Street, Summerhill, Dimmock Street, Bell Street, Wesley Avenue, Bailor Street, Pittsburgh, Houston Street, Storrs, and Carrie Steele. These schools were led by some of Atlanta's leading educators, including Bazoline Usher (Ashby Street School), M. Agnes Jones (Summerhill), and Cora B. Finley (Yonge Street).

The Atlanta Board of Education had eliminated the eighth grade from all of its public schools in 1915, and white students graduating from the seventh grade then went directly to high school. Since there were no high schools for blacks in Atlanta (and only three in the state), the students would suffer from this change. In 1917, the Atlanta School Board made further plans to eliminate the seventh grade for African-American students. There were numerous private schools that charged fees, including Our Lady of Lourdes Catholic School, St. Paul Parish School, Holmes Institute, and the schools that the colleges provided, but there was still a grave need for public education.

The fledgling Atlanta chapter of the NAACP sent a six-man committee to protest the situation. The committee gained the support of board member James L. Key, who would later become mayor, and the board backed down. The NAACP pushed a letter-writing campaign to the school board asking for the elimination of the double shift, a common practice in all fourteen of Atlanta's black schools. Some teachers taught sixty pupils from 8:30 to noon and sixty more from 12:30 to 4:00. The old dilapidated wooden school buildings could not accommodate all who wanted to attend. Black Atlantans began to demand better buildings, a junior high school for industrial education, and a high school. Because of the success of the NAACP voter registration drive and voter boycott of the 1919 bond election, black leaders made it known to the board that unless a black high school was promised in advance of the election, they would use their influence to have African-American voters vote against the bonds. As a result, the first high school and several elementary schools were acquired. The success of this feat had come through after black Atlantans regrouped from having twice voted down two school bond issues which prevented the schools from being constructed. A Democratic white primary barred blacks from voting where it counted. Black leaders once again called an eleventh hour mass meeting. Massive efforts to register voters helped to pass a 1921 bond referendum making possible the construction of William Crogman, David T. Howard, E.P. Johnson, and E.A. Ware Elementary Schools and Booker T. Washington High School.

The curriculum of education shared the basics, but not the specifics of African-American history. It was unthinkable that it be taught as a subject. Carter G. Woodson's Association of Negro Life and History in 1926 would introduce the history of African Americans during the third week in February.

Members of the faculty posed for this photograph following the dedication of the statue of Booker T. Washington in front of the high school named for him in 1924. The first class graduated in 1927 and consisted of about one hundred fifty students. In 1928, Lena Horne enrolled at Washington High School and became one of thousands who would pass through its doors, including Martin Luther King Jr. Seated directly in the center, beginning tenth from left, are: Assistant Principal Professor Charles N. Cornell; Principal Professor Charles Harper; and English teacher Mrs. Louie D. Shivery, author of the school's Alma Mater. (Digging It Up Archives.)

Prior to the construction of new schools in the 1920s, black children attended old dilapidated schools such as the Roach Street School. (*The Black Side* by E.R. Carter.)

The Mitchell Street School was eventually closed, and students in the area were redirected to attend the E.A. Ware School, *c*. 1920. (Digging It Up Archives.)

The Ashby Street School opened in 1919 with Charles Walter Hill serving as principal. He was followed by Hattie Landrum Green, who served as principal from 1919 to 1928. Miss Bessie E. Smith succeeded Mrs. Green. The school was renamed E.R. Carter Elementary School in 1946. (Digging It Up Archives.)

Ms. Harriet Randolph Bailey posed with her class at the Ashby Street School, c. 1920s. (Digging It Up Archives.)

This unidentified club at Booker T. Washington High School posed for this photograph c. 1927. (Digging It Up Archives.)

The original Summerhill School on Martin Street was demolished in 1922 to make way for the new school, which would be named for Rev. E.P. Johnson. (*The Black Side* by E.R. Carter.)

The Edwin P. Johnson School was constructed in 1923 on the corner of Fulton and Martin Streets and was named for Rev. E.P. Johnson, pastor of Reed Street Baptist Church. The school replaced the old Summer Hill School. (Digging It Up Archives.)

Though not a public school, the Carrie Steele Orphanage had a history of providing social welfare to the children of Atlanta since 1899, when Carrie Steele, a maid at the Union Depot, began to take care of and provide for homeless and parentless children. In May of 1928, the orphanage moved to this site on Roy Street near Memorial Drive. Mrs. Clara Pitts, who began working at the facility in 1917, became the manager and treasurer after the death of Miss Steele. The orphanage was aided greatly by the Atlanta Community Chest. (Clara Hayley.)

Seven
Where We Worked

Many African-American men found work as porters, bellmen, doormen, and servers in downtown Atlanta hotels such as the Henry Grady, the Biltmore, and the Imperial. This doorman worked at one of the hotels, c. 1920s. (Digging It Up Archives.)

H.C. Thornton (left) and Lucious Henderson (right) operated a photography studio out of the home of Henderson on Martin Street in the Summerhill community. Henderson was born in Washington, Georgia, in 1886. He moved to Atlanta around 1916, and worked for another photographer before establishing his own shop. He was said to have been a practicing Israelite and usually wore a cap to cover the long hair that he never cut. (Digging It Up Archives.)

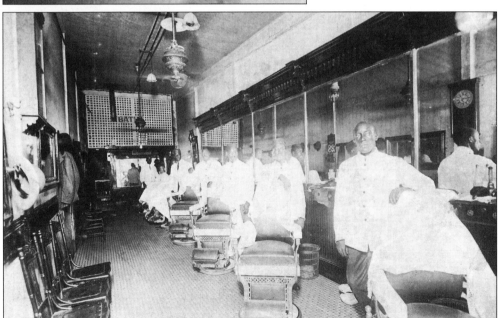

Shorter's Barber Shop was established in 1912 on Decatur Street. By 1924, there were several other black businesses on the street, including A.D. Mayfield, Walton, Farmer Barbershops, Kings and Brown Restaurants, and the 81 and 91 Theaters. (Haroldeen Crowder/Digging It Up Archives.)

Many African-American men worked in the locomotive repair shops of the rail yards of the Macon and West Railroad companies in the Mechanicsville community. (Digging It Up Archives.)

Dr. Loring B. Palmer, son of Fred and Julia Palmer, had an interesting family history. His father was a white pharmacist at Jacob's Pharmacy who created a skin whitening cream. He fell in love with Julia, an African-American woman, and created a stir in Atlanta, where interracial relationships were prohibited. Fred Palmer died in 1919. The Palmers resided on Mitchell Street. (Ella Gaines Yates.)

Dr. Georgia Dwelle was born in Albany, Georgia, in 1883 to Rev. George H. Dwelle, former pastor of Springfield Church in Augusta, Georgia. She studied at Walker Baptist Institute and entered Spelman Seminary, where she graduated. She pursued her medical degree at Meharry Medical College in Nashville, Tennessee, and graduated with honors in 1904. In 1906, Dr. Dwelle moved to Atlanta and practiced obstetrics and pediatrics. She established Dwelle Infirmary, where many babies were born. She was also vice-president of the National Medical Association in 1923, and was a member of the Women's Christian Temperance Union and the National Association of Colored Women. Dr. Georgia Dwelle Rooks Johnson died on July 28, 1977. (Digging It Up Archives.)

The Dwelle Infirmary was located on Boulevard. It closed in 1949 and was reopened as the Beaumont School of Nursing. (*Sage* magazine, Spelman College.)

Mercy Hospital was located on Yonge Street next to the Yonge Street School, a public school for African-American children. It was completely staffed by African-American nurses. R.L. Goodrum, the African-American hardware store magnate lived on Yonge near the hospital. (Margaret Jacobs.)

One of the nurses at Mercy Hospital was Sudie Shelton Aiken (left), shown with Ola Fredericks (right) and an unidentified nurse, in front of the hospital. Mrs. Aiken came to Atlanta in 1909 from Alexander City, Alabama, and is believed to have received her training at the Atlanta Medical College. In 1919, she was hired as director of the hospital. (Margaret Jacobs.)

Dr. Hamilton Holmes Sr., a native of Marksville, Louisiana, came to Atlanta in 1910 and set up his medical practice in East Point and Atlanta. He began his practice in Atlanta in 1923 and was a member of the board of directors for the Citizens Trust Bank. Holmes was an avid golfer and a charter member of the Atlanta chapter of Kappa Alpha Psi Fraternity, along with A.B. Cooper, James E. Stamps, J.R. Pinkett, B.H. Gentry, G.E. Wilson, and Brothers Graham and Owens. The chapter was chartered on February 27, 1924. (Alice Holmes Washington.)

This is an advertisement for Dr. Fred Palmer's Skin Whitener cream, which was sold at Jacob's Pharmacy. It was one of the most popular skin creams. The ad appeared in most black newspapers and magazines.

Dr. A.B. Cooper's dental office over the Yates and Milton Drug Store in the Odd Fellows Auditorium was in a building with other doctors: Antoine Graves, A.D. Jones, R.B. Jackson, H.D. Canady, J.W.E. Linder, G.A. Howell, C.W. Powell, and A.G. Taylor. Cooper's advertisement proclaimed that "Teeth were extracted by the nerve blocking method." (Mrs. Ann B. Cooper.)

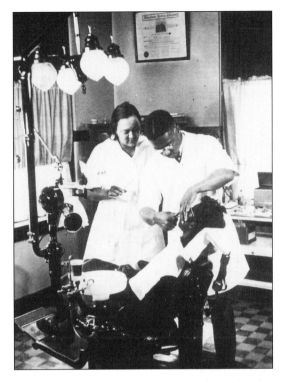

Mrs. Ludie Andrews had a stellar career as a nurse. She graduated from Spelman's Nurses Training Course in 1906 and worked as the superintendent of the Lula Grove Hospital Training School. In 1914, she organized a class of African-American nurses and started the Training School for Colored Nurses at Grady Hospital. It was chartered in 1917. In 1919, she became the first African-American registered nurse in Georgia. In 1920, the first class graduated after three years of work to have the school accredited. Nurse Andrews also served as the nurse for Morehouse College and at the McVicar Hospital at Spelman College, where she also taught hygiene and nursing classes. In addition, she was president of the Neighborhood Union. (Margaret Jacobs.)

Dr. Homer E. Nash was a native of White Plains, Georgia. He graduated from Meharry Medical College in 1910, came to Atlanta following graduation, and established his practice there. He served two years in World War I as a medical doctor in France and at Camp Gordon in DeKalb County before being discharged in March of 1919. He then reopened his office on Auburn Avenue, where he remained until his retirement. In the 1920s, he built a home on Simpson Road for his wife, Marie Graves Nash, and their six children. (Harriet Nash Chisholm.)

In this photograph, Dr. and Mrs. Henry Rutherford Butler enjoy collecting shells at an unidentified location. Dr. Butler came to Atlanta in the 1870s. During the 1920s, he continued to serve as the grand master of the Prince Hall Masonic lodge, a position he had held since 1902 and would hold until his death in 1932. Butler was also director of the Fair Haven Hospital on Irwin Street, associated with Morris Brown, and had an office in the newly constructed Herndon Building. The Depression caused a substantial decrease in membership from 24,000 to about 2,500. Mrs. Butler was a member of the YWCA, the founder of the National Congress of Colored Parent and Teachers Association in 1923, and member of the Sigma Gamma Rho Sorority. (Digging It Up Archives.)

Nurses Julia Johnson (left) and Lizzie Malone are pictured in front of the Harris Hospital on Hunter Street, c. 1920. The hospital was established by Sadye Lillian Harris Powell, a native of Atlanta who graduated from Spelman College and matriculated at Providence Hospital in Chicago, Illinois, where she received her nurse training in 1912. She married C.W. Powell, and they established the William A. Harris Memorial Hospital. (Wynelle Hannon/Digging It Up Archives.)

Here, Dr. Thomas Heathe Slater is pictured with his doctor's bag beside his car. Dr. Slater came to Atlanta in 1888 after completing his studies at Meharry Medical College. He co-founded the Gate City Drug Store with Moses Amos and served as one of Atlanta's leading African-American physicians. He was also a member of the Kappa Boule of Sigma Pi Phi, the 27 Club, and Alpha Phi Alpha Fraternity. (Digging It Up Archives.)

Front Row, from left to right: Mesdames R. H. Carter, R. E. Mattison, H. E. Nash, H. M. Holmes, A. B. Cooper, H. D. Canady, Jr., G. B. Warren, N. Lamar and S. M. Lewis.
Back Row, left to right: Mesdames Joe Hamilton, Wm. Burney, J. W. Madison, R. M. Reddick, Jno. W. Burney, B. M. Sherard, C. W. Powell, Ward Weaver, T. C. Jones, Chas. H. Johnson, J. W. E. Linder, and E. R. Martin.

Mrs. H. M. Holmes
President

H. D. Canady, Jr., M. D.
Chairman, Local Program

G. A. Howell, M. D.
Chr., Assemblage Committee

We wish to take this means to thank this congenial group of women for their very excellent support.
G. A. Howell,
H. D. Canady, Jr., Chairmen.

The National Medical Association, which had been founded in Atlanta in 1895 held its national convention in Atlanta in 1928. This is a page from the souvenir booklet. (Alice Holmes Washington.)

In the fall of 1912, Henry Ivey (shown here) and his brother, James, established the Ivey Brothers Funeral Home on Walker and Peters Streets. In 1920, they relocated to 492 Larkin Street, where the building still stands, though it has been renamed the Carl Williams Funeral Home, after the death of Ivey's daughter Clara Ivey Wilson, who operated the funeral home. (Digging It Up Archives.)

David T. Howard (center), with wife Ella, their children, and grandchildren, celebrated their fiftieth wedding anniversary in 1920. Born a slave in Crawford, Georgia, Howard moved to Atlanta and established himself as one of the most successful undertakers in the city, amassing substantial wealth and prestige. Howard's Funeral Home entered the 1920s with a brand new hearse at its location on Piedmont Avenue. (Digging It Up Archives.)

There were only three African-American attorneys in Atlanta in the 1920s. One of them was Col. Thomas W. Holmes, a former mail carrier. Born in Washington, Georgia, Holmes attended Atlanta University and "read law" with Peyton Allen. He passed the bar in 1912. Holmes's most famous client was middleweight boxing champion Tiger Flowers. Father of two daughters, Louise and Grace, Holmes was a member of the First Congregational Church. (Grace Holmes DeLorme.)

Peyton Allen graduated from Atlanta University and established himself as an outspoken advocate for civil rights prior to being admitted to the Georgia Bar. He was charter member of the Atlanta chapter of the NAACP. Allen was born in Blackshear, Georgia, in the late 1880s, and was a successful educator who taught in Perry, Georgia, and later assumed the principalship of the Mitchell Street School. (The Herndon Foundation.)

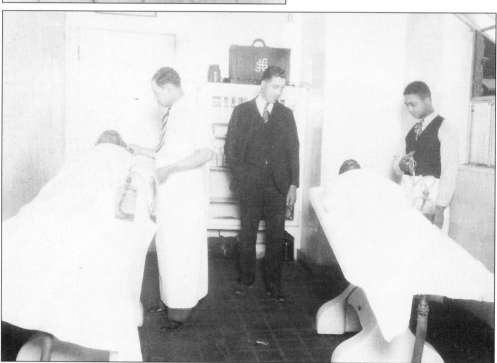

These are embalmers of Hanley's Bell Street Funeral Home, c. 1928.

Eight
Where We Lived

African Americans in Atlanta found themselves residing in one of numerous African-American neighborhoods in the city. These included Summerhill, Mechanicsville, Rockdale, Peoplestown, the Atlanta University area, Darktown, Jenningstown, South Atlanta, Ashley Heights, Washington Park, Buttermilk Bottom, Lightning, the Westside, Tanyard Bottom, Macedonia Park in Buckhead, Vine City, Reynoldstown, and the Old Fourth Ward. During the 1920s, some of the black middle class of Atlanta lived in the Boulevard area of the Old Fourth Ward, Washington Park, Hunter Hills, and the Atlanta University Center. On Boulevard near Morris Brown was an area where many of the leading doctors, ministers, and bishops resided, including attorney Thomas W. Holmes and Dr. John W. Burney, who resided in the home above. In 1940s, Rev. Martin Luther King Sr. and his family would occupy the home.

The Herndon Home in the Vine City section was the site of many "swanky" parties, elegant luncheons and teas, and other social affairs during the decade of the 1920s. Norris Herndon often hosted his fraternity at the home, and Mrs. Jessie Herndon hosted her club meetings as well as Atlanta Life Insurance functions. It was constructed in 1910 by Alonzo Herndon and his first wife, Adrienne. (The Herndon Foundation.)

Several families lived here, including Dr. Fred Palmer, inventor of Palmer Skin Whitening Cream; Dr. W.A. Fountain, AME bishop and president of Morris Brown College; and Dr. Hamilton Holmes Sr. Located on Boulevard in the Old Fourth Ward section, the home was demolished in 1995 by the Georgia Baptist Hospital and is now used for parking. (Digging It Up Archives.)

Shown here is the home of the president of Morehouse College, John Hope and his wife, Lugenia Burns Hope, and their sons Edward and John, on the campus of Morehouse on the West Side of Atlanta near Fair Street. Several prominent persons resided on Fair Street, including Charles Wardlaw, photographer R.E. Hood, Dr. C.W. Reeves, printer Harry S. Murphy, and Morehouse Coach B.T. Harvey. Flipper Temple AME and Mt. Carmel Baptist Churches were also on Fair Street. (Digging It Up Archives.)

During the 1920s, William and Mabel Driskell, founders of Dermis Cura Hair Preparation School, lived in this home on the corner of Ashby Street and Ashby Grove. The house was torn down in 1941 and was replaced by the Warren Memorial Methodist Church. (Margaret Jacobs.)

The palatial mansion of boxer Theodore "Tiger" Flowers was constructed by the Aiken and Faulkner Construction Company in 1926. The house had a large living room, music room, sun parlor, billiard room, dining room, breakfast room, and kitchen (with an electric dishwasher) on the first floor, with five bedrooms and two baths upstairs. The furnishings for the house were selected from Stephen Philibosian, Inc. The floors were hardwood, with parquet flooring downstairs. In the rear of the house was a combination gymnasium and three-car garage. When the house was completed, it was opened to the public. "Tiger's" death on November 16, 1927,

following an operation in a New York Sanitarium, shocked the world, especially his hometown of Atlanta. When his body was returned from New York and placed in state at his palatial home on Simpson Road, thousands of citizens, both black and white, lined up for blocks to pay final respects to him. From the 1930s to the 1950s, the house was owned by the Jones family, another black family, who rented it out for parties, weddings, and receptions. It was demolished in 1961 to build Fire Station No. 16, the station to house African-American firemen. (Digging It Up Archives.)

Between Piedmont Avenue and Boulevard was "Buttermilk Bottom," a vibrant, ragged neighborhood for black Atlantans, both poor and middle class. The name might have come from the smell of rotten buttermilk caused by a battery factory or some industrial use of acid in the area. Buttermilk Bottom was located near the Bedford Pines area. The area was cleared during the urban renewal of the 1960s.

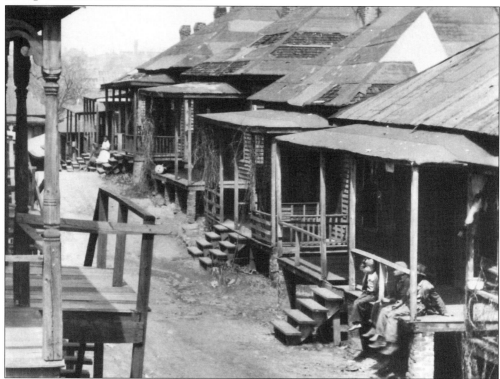

These homes, located in the slums of the Beaver Run area near Spelman College, would later be demolished and replaced by the John Hope Homes and University Homes Public Housing projects.

The home of Howard and Clara Pitts and
Clayton and Mae Yates and family on Markham
Street, near Maple and Hunter Streets in the
Vine City community, is pictured here c. 1920.
The neighborhood was near the " Lightning"
and Jenningstown sections of the city.
(Clara Hayley.)

Pictured here is the Lucious Henderson
Home on Martin Street in the
Summerhill community, c. 1920.
Summerhill was Atlanta's oldest
predominately African-American
community, and it was established in
the 1860s, after the Civil War. (Digging
It Up Archives.)

The Walker Home was located on Ashby Street in the Ashby Heights section, a very fashionable residential neighborhood partially developed by Heman Perry. One of the residents during the 1920s included Rev. King H. Burris, founder of the Bethlehem Church of God in Christ, c. 1920. (Walter Reid.)

Auburn Avenue had a mixture of residential housing and businesses. These two houses are typical of the homes located in the block of Auburn between Jackson Street and Boulevard during the 1920s. In the next block, between Boulevard and Howell Street, resided many pioneering and prominent African Americans, including Moses W. Calhoun, Bishop Lucious Holsey, Wesley C. Redding, Rev. A.D. Williams, Charles L. Harper, Antoine Graves, Charles Faison, and Sylvia Bryant's School. (Digging It Up Archives.)

Nine
Arts and Entertainment

As the pages of *Opportunity* and *Crisis* burned with the literary works of Countee Cullen, Langston Hughes, and Zora Neale Hurston, James A. Hopkins Bookstore on Auburn Avenue was the only such outlet to obtain these literary works in Atlanta. Also contributing to the flavor of the renaissance was Georgia Douglass Johnson, a 1893 graduate of Atlanta University. Johnson, who married Henry Lincoln Johnson, a major black Republican political figure and lawyer, published three volumes of poetry reflecting the life and psyche of African-American women. Atlanta's cultural scene was vibrant also. Atlanta boasted many artists, musicians, writers, and poets, including Welborn V. Jenkins (right). Jenkins was one of the most prolific writers in Atlanta. His works were featured in the *Atlanta Independent* newspaper and *The Crisis* magazine. Born in 1879, Jenkins's works included two books of poetry: *Trumpet in the New Moon and Other Poems, Who are the Thespians?* and *The "Incident" at Monroe.* Jenkins founded a monthly periodical he called *The Colored Peoples Magazine,* which catered to the cultural and literary side of African-American life. It was published by the Auburn Publishing Company.(Digging It Up Archives.)

Thomas Jefferson Flanigan's poetry and prose began to appear in the *Atlanta Independent* newspaper and the Atlanta University publication *The Scroll*, the journal of Atlanta University which he edited. Flanigan graduated from Atlanta University in 1927. (Digging It Up Archives.)

In this photograph, friends gather for a summer afternoon of fun and frolic. From left to right are: (front row) Rosa Harris; (middle row) Laura Moore Gaines, Lee, Sadye Harris, Mitchell, and William Powell; (back row) Loring Palmer and Lee. Rosa Harris married Loring Palmer. Her sister, Sadye Harris, married William Powell. They established the William Harris Memorial Hospital in 1927. (Ella Gaines Yates.)

Mae Maxwell Yates, a graduate of Atlanta University, worked with the Urban League during the 1920s and with her husband, Clayton Yates, in the chain of Yates and Milton Drug Stores. She was a member of the Kappa Omega Chapter of Alpha Kappa Alpha Sorority and also the Chatauqua Circle, one of the oldest literary clubs in Atlanta. Her mother, Clara Cater Pitts, was a founder of the Atlanta chapter of the Sigma Gamma Rho Sorority and managed the Carrie Steele orphanage. (Clara Hayley.)

The Junior Matrons Club was one of hundreds of social and civic clubs consisting of African-American women in Atlanta. From left to right are: (seated) Josephine Murphy; (standing) Maudeline Reynolds, Lula Partee, Vonziel Burch, unidentified, Beulah Lewis (founding chair of the Colored Division of the American Cancer Society), unidentified, Helen Martin, and unidentified, c. 1927.

J. Neal Montgomery (seated), pictured here surrounded by members of his band, performed at many dances and parties in Atlanta. Montgomery taught at Booker T. Washington High School and later David T. Howard High School. He established the Southeastern Artists Bureau, an entertainment booking company. Montgomery was responsible for bringing many major acts to Atlanta, from Duke Ellington to Louis Armstrong. (Digging It Up Archives.)

The vaudeville palace of Atlanta for African Americans was the 81 Theater, located at 81 Decatur Street. The theater opened in 1913 and was owned and operated by the Bailey brothers, Charles and Tom. The Baileys also owned several other theaters, including the Ashby Theater on Hunter Street and the Royal Theater on Auburn Avenue. Gut-wrenching blues singers such as Sara Martin, who recorded "Atlanta Blues" on Okeh Records, sang here, and vaudeville and comedic acts also blazed the stage of the theater. (Digging It Up Archives.)

Gertrude "Ma" Rainey began performing at the 81 Theater in her teens with her band known as the Black Bottom Band and the the Rabbit Foot Minstrels. She called everyone "honey" and "baby." Born Gertrude Pridgett in Columbus, Georgia, she had a colorful career. During her stints at the 81 Theater, she befriended Villa Rica and Georgia native Thomas Dorsey, who was known as Georgia Tom. He joined her band, arranged her music, and recorded records with her until 1928. (Digging It Up Archives.)

Bessie Smith was a regular performer at the 81 and 91 Theaters on Decatur Street. On February 15, 1923, Bessie recorded "Down Home Blues" at Columbia's studio in New York. The record was a hit and sold 780,000 copies in the first six months. Bessie only made $125 from the record. That same year, she married Jack Gee, a night watchman from Atlanta, who also became her manager. (Digging It Up Archives.)

Shown here standing in front of the 81 Theater is Butterbean (of Butterbean and Susie) and pianist Eddie Heywood Sr (right). Heywood was the house pianist for the 81 Theater, along with Ed Butler and Graham Jackson. (Lottie Heywood Watkins.)

Neal Montgomery (standing) also directed the Collegiate Ramblers, shown on the stage of the 81 Theater. The band consisted of students from several schools, including Clark University. (Digging It Up Archives.)

Graham Jackson and members of the Dixie Melody Syncopators ride on board a truck advertising Atlanta's home-grown Coca-Cola. The truck is in front of the Coca-Cola Bottling Plant on Auburn Avenue, *c.* 1927. (Digging It Up Archives.)

The students at Booker T. Washington High School under the direction of Graham Jackson presented the musical theatrical production *Once in a Blue Moon*, an operetta in three acts, at the City Auditorium in May of 1926. (Digging It Up Archives.)

WEEK COMMENCING MONDAY, SEPTEMBER 13th

TIGER FLOWERS
MIDDLEWEIGHT CHAMPION OF THE WORLD
in the most sensational movie film ever screened

"The Fighting Deacon"

SPECIAL ADDED ALL-STAR VAUDEVILLE CAST

BROWN & BROWN
DANCING, SINGING & COMEDY SKETCH

JENNINGS & REED
CREOLE MUSICAL NOVELTY ACT

VADER & HUNTER
THE FAST STEPPERS

KIRKPATRICK & BOWMAN
IN A LITTLE ACT ALL THEIR OWN

ALSO ANOTHER HIGH-CLASS SURPRISE ACT

WEEK OF SEPTEMBER 20th

IRVIN C. MILLER'S

"RED HOT MAMMA"

Direct from a long run at Lafayette Theater, N. Y.

BIG MIDNITE SHOW SUNDAY NITE

A movie was made on the life of "Tiger" Flowers in 1927, following his championship win. The movie played at African-American theaters throughout the country. Flowers's middleweight boxing title came as a result of a decision in a fight between Harry Greb and him on February 26, 1927 at Madison Square Garden in New York. He returned to Atlanta a hero. (Reprint from the *Chicago Defender* newspaper.)

Ten

Theodore "Tiger" Flowers

Atlanta's First Black Sports Champion

"Personally, I never have considered pugilism, the highest form of human entertainment. At the same time I must confess that, as compared with the soldiers, the pugilist ranks high in my set of values. I think that fighting with padded fists under set rules of fairness and with some limits to the punishment that may be inflicted is infinitely to be preferred to modern warfare in any aspects."
W.E.B. DuBois, *Pittsburgh Courier*, 1923

During the 1920s, young African-American males did not have many sports heroes. That would soon change when a former WW I shipyard worker in Philadelphia, boxer Theodore Flowers, would make Atlanta his home and in turn create an aura and legacy so strong that both races in Atlanta would forget his color and would espouse the words of Benjamin E. Mays, who said, "You make your living by what you do and you make your life by what you give." (Digging It Up Archives.)

Theodore "Tiger" Flowers

Flowers was born in February 1894 to sharecropping parents Aaron and Lula Flowers in the small southwest Georgia town of Camilla. At the age of six, his family moved to Brunswick, Georgia, where he attended Risley School and the Seldon Institute. His muscular, sculpted build had not come from weight training, but from his years as a call boy, stevedore, boilermaker, porter, steel riveter, laborer on a subway that was being constructed in Philadelphia, and in the shipyards constructing ships during World War One. (Digging It Up Archives.)

Theodore "Tiger" Flowers was Atlanta's 1920s renaissance man. He was an immaculate dresser, a generous philanthropist, and a ferocious boxer. He arrived in Atlanta during the height of Atlanta's political insurgency and racial transition in the 1920s. He was 5'11 and weighed 160 pounds. He was a dancer who moved so fast in buck-and-wing dances that he developed his legs and arms. Flowers's exterior dexterity could not match his interior soul and heart. Though he was soft spoken, he had a punch so powerful he was given the nickname "Tiger." With a Bible clutched in one hand, a Bengal tiger on the back of his robe, and the 144th verse of Psalm in his mouth, "Blessed be the Lord, my strength, which teacheth my hands to war and fingers to fight," Atlanta, the South, and the country fell in love with this sports figure. Black children would hail him as hero, black men called him an idol, and white men would exclaim that he was the "Whitest black man in the ring," a reference to his humble and clean style of fighting. (William Calloway.)

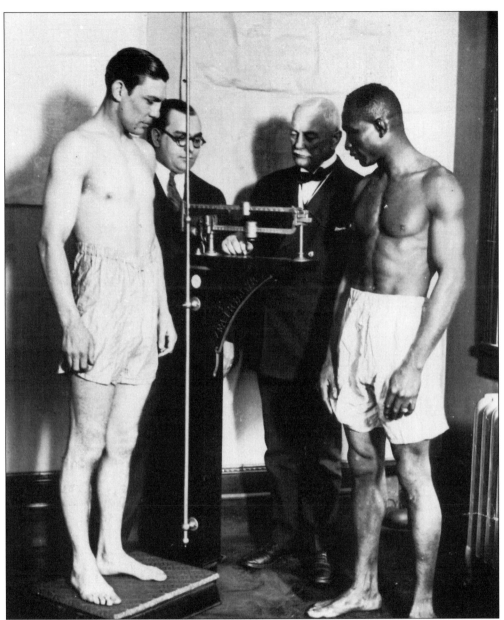

Here, Flowers is shown at a weigh-in, with Harry Greb on the scale. On February 26, 1926, a crowd of over two thousand packed the newly renovated Madison Square Garden to watch Flowers fight Harry Greb in a middleweight championship bout. After thirteen rounds, the fight ended in a draw, and "Tiger" was given the decision and became the first African-American middleweight champion of the world. He returned to Atlanta to a hero's welcome and all of the fame and fortune awarded to a champion, including a parade and banquet.

Flowers's career was stellar, with a record of 149 bouts and 49 knock outs. On December 3, 1926, "Tiger" lost the title to Mickey Walker in a fight that was called one of the worst decisions in boxing history. Even in defeat, "Tiger" attempted to hug his opponent, an act consistent with Flowers in every fight. Walk Miller, Flowers's manager, demanded a rematch. (Digging it Up Archives.)

For boxing enthusiasts, vivid memories of the antics and escapades of boxing's first black heavyweight champion, Jack Johnson, were still etched in their minds. Johnson's verbosity, his love for white women, his flamboyance and flashiness, and his innate ability to punch the daylights out of white boxers made him a threat to many whites. "Tiger" was just the opposite. He joined Butler Street CME Church in December of 1923 with his wife, Willie Mae (his childhood sweetheart), and became a member of the Steward Board. His generosity to the church led to purchasing of new pews. He also gave generously to the black colleges in Atlanta. Here, "Tiger" is shown with Jack Johnson (third from right) following a banquet in "Tiger's" honor in Chicago at the Ambassador Club, where he was made an honorary member. Entertainer Eubie Blake was present and played a few selections., c. 1926. (Lewis Jay/Digging It Up Archives.)

"Tiger" (seated) is pictured with his friend and fellow boxer "Bear" Lawson in this c. 1920 portrait.

The constant punching from boxing caused scar tissue and eye damage to "Tiger," which, after a series of car accidents, made it necessary for him to have surgery. The operation was performed by Dr. William Fralic in Harlem, but "Tiger" died after coming out of the ether. His sudden death created grief and shock throughout the world. The funeral of "Tiger" Flowers was held at the City Auditorium on Courtland Street on November 17, 1926, to accommodate the throngs of persons who wanted to attend. His church, Butler Street CME Church, was too small to handle the massive crowd. Rev. G.L. Word preached the eulogy and Kemper Harreld, famed

musician and instructor at Morehouse and Spelman provided music. It was the first time in the history of Atlanta that an African-American funeral was held in the facility. White mourners lined the balcony as the blacks sat on the floor of the auditorium. Thousands more lined the streets after the funeral as the procession headed to Lincoln Cemetery, where he was buried. Flowers's funeral was the greatest display of respect and humanity Atlanta had ever witnessed, and the city would not witness such a display again until the funeral of Rev. Dr. Martin Luther King some forty-one years later in 1968. (Atlanta History Center.)

It was estimated that "Tiger" earned over half a million dollars in his career. He owned several pieces of property and numerous cars. Here, his manager, Walk Miller, stands over the gold-plated casket, an exact replica of the casket used for Harlem Renaissance dancer Florence Mills, who had died a few weeks before "Tiger." Before his body was shipped to Atlanta, thousands stood in the rain to view his remains at the Howell Funeral Home in Harlem. Even more would line the streets of Simpson Road back to Ashby to pay their last respects. Cards and floral arrangements came from many boxers, including Jack Dempsey and others. Boxing trophies and the middleweight title belt adorned the bier of his casket. "Tiger" was survived by his mother, father, wife Willie Mae, and daughter Verna. (Atlanta History Center.)

In this photograph, undertaker Jesse Hanley (in the rear), a close friend of "Tiger," supervises the removal of the casket from the home as members of "Tiger's" Masonic lodge served as pallbearers. Flowers was buried in Lincoln Cemetery, on Simpson Road. Shortly after his death, singer Porter Grainger recorded a song, "He's Gone Home," for Columbia records. Flowers's mother, Lula, was also buried in Lincoln Cemetery a few years later. Today, a granite bench and memorial mark his grave. (Atlanta History Center.)

Eleven

Atlanta University

"When the Crimson and Gray banner waves its victory,
True and loyal sons, Atlanta, We'll come back to thee"

Words from the Alma Mater by G. Floyd Zimmerman

Atlanta had the unique factor of having five colleges and universities for African-American students. Though founded at different times and in different areas, these schools comprised the Atlanta University Center, the largest consortium of African-American colleges and universities in the country. During the 1920s, all of the schools were still in their infancy in developing their college curricula. Most of the schools offered private elementary and high school courses. By the end of the 1920s, the schools had redeveloped their scope and foci.

Atlanta University was founded in 1865. By the decade of the 1920s, "AU" was experiencing rapid growth and change simultaneously. In 1927, the Atlanta University choir recorded the "Negro National Anthem" on Columbia Records. Atlanta University would abandon the above campus and move closer to Morehouse and Spelman, which it merged with in 1929 to form Atlanta University Center. Morris Brown University would occupy the campus and lease it from "AU."

Fellow classmates paused for this picture. Note Bumstead Cottage and the Herndon Home in the far background, c. 1924. The Atlanta University campus was located on a 48-acre tract of land acquired from Edward Parson in 1869 and bounded by Hunter, Chestnut, Parsons, and Tatnall Streets. The area was known as Diamond Hill.

To the friends of the Open Door:

THE message of the Pageant will quicken sympathetic interest in the progress of the Negro people, and remind us that the same aspirations are at the heart of all forward looking people. You are striking a blow and singing a song for democracy. You are helping toward a larger Christian fellowship."

From a letter of President Ware

"The Open Door"

A Pageant commemorating the 50th Anniversary of

ATLANTA UNIVERSITY

For fifty years an Open Door for the Negro youth of America.

SYMPHONY HALL

Wednesday Evening, December the 8th, 1920

At Eight O'Clock

Students at Atlanta University presented the pageant *The Open Door* at the Symphony Hall to white audiences to celebrate the fiftieth anniversary of the founding of the school. The pageant consisted of a cast of over 150, with a chorus of 150, a symphony, and special lighting effects.

The *c.* 1923 Atlanta University Football team, was coached by "Chief" Walter Aiken (second row, far right), a graduate of Howard University. Some of the players pictured are Booker T. McGraw (front row, fifth from left), Henry Lang (front row, sixth from left), and W.C. Thomas (front row, seventh from left).

Pictured here is the cover of *The Scroll*, the Atlanta University magazine of ideas and thoughts, from April 1925.

Seated in the center of the members of *The Scroll* board is Thomas Jefferson Flanagan, editor, *c.* 1925.

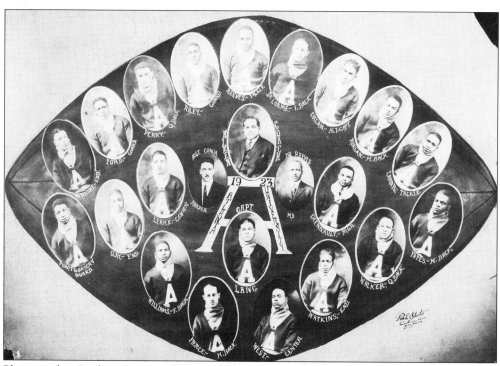

Photographer Paul Poole created a composite of the 1923 Atlanta University Football team. The AU Tigers were one of the most formidable teams in the state. In 1927, the school installed an electric scoreboard, the first of its kind. (Atlanta History Center.)

One of the most talented and illustrious graduates of Atlanta University was Fletcher "Smack" Henderson, a chemistry major and 1920 graduate who left Atlanta for New York to work on a Master's degree and became one of the most respected bandleaders in the country. Henderson got his start at the Club Alabama and is credited for creating the syncopated jazz rhythms. Both Louis Armstrong and former Atlantan Lena Horne performed with Henderson's band. While at AU, he played the pipe organ and played football. (Digging It Up Archives.)

Shown here are the Episcopal church college students at Atlanta University, March 1925. (Father Henry J.C. Bowden.)

Here, the charter members of the Alpha Beta Chapter of Alpha Kappa Alpha Sorority at Atlanta University pose on the steps of the home of Mrs. Jane Evans, the chapter advisor and member of the local Atlanta chapter. The chapter was founded in 1923 and included Grace Towns Hamilton (second row, far right), who became executive secretary of the National Urban League and Georgia's first African-American female state legislator. (Digging It Up Archives.)

Pictured above are members of the Kappa Omega Chapter of Alpha Kappa Alpha Sorority in 1926. The local Atlanta chapter was chartered in March 1923. Their first Silver Tea was held in January of 1924. Members in 1924 (not shown) were Ruth Greenwood Carey, Claudia White Harreld, Louie D. Shivery, Jessie Mae Quarles, Flaxie Pinkett, Helen Chandler, Madeline Smith Davis, Marie Taylor, Hilda Johnson Evans, Sarah Flemister, Virginia Graham, Mildred Greenwood, Susie Williams Jones, and Bertha Keith. By 1926, Mae Yates (standing on the back row at far left) was a member. Many of its members were graduates of Atlanta University or employed by the school. (Reprint from the *Ivy Leaf*, 1926.)

Pictured here are the charter members of Delta Sigma Theta Sorority at Atlanta University, c. 1923. From left to right are: Lula Brown, Florence Phelps, Hazel Shanks, Louise Holmes, Mattie Owens, Sarah Brimmer, Ruth Wheeler, Doris Pace, Altona Trent Johns, and Minnie Perry.

The Pyramid Club of Delta Sigma Theta Sorority at Atlanta University posed for this photograph c. 1930. Pictured are, from left to right: (front row) H. Ball, E. Baker, O. Moore, and C. Mabry; (back row) N. Johnson, M. Reed, E. Christler, V. Davie, and B. Johnson. When the Atlanta University became solely a graduate school, the fraternities and sororities disbanded.

Roscoe Edwin Thomas graduated from Atlanta University and went on to law school. He founded the law firm Thomas, Kennedy, Sampson and Patterson, one of the oldest surviving African-American law firms in Atlanta. (Marnie Thomas.)

The Atlanta University Drama Department's annual Shakespearean presentation is shown here, c. 1922.

Twelve

Clark University

Clark University was situated in the "South Atlanta" area. It was bounded by McDonough Boulevard and Jonesboro Road. Founded in 1869 by the Freedman's Aid Society of the Methodist Episcopal Church, the University's first location was at Whitehall and McDaniel Street. Bishop Henry W. Warren secured a tract of land of between 400 and 500 acres in South Atlanta, and the school was moved in 1872. A large portion of the funds for the school were contributed by Mrs. Augusta Clark Cole, the daughter of Bishop D.W. Clark, who died in 1872. The school was named in the memory of the Clark family.

Some of the most visually well-crafted architecture in Atlanta was found on the South Atlanta campus of Clark University, including Crogman Chapel and Leete Hall. Crogman Chapel accommodated eight hundred persons. Crogman also contained a gymnasium, administrative offices, and classrooms, including science and biology labs. In 1920, the foundations were laid for Leete Hall (seen here), a structure costing over $200,000. It was dedicated February 15, 1922. The building is now used as the George Washington Carver High School.

Matthew Simpson Davage brought Clark University into the decade of the 1920s when he was named president in 1924. He had graduated from New Orleans University and did graduate work at the University of Chicago and Columbia University. Davage served at George Smith College, Haven Institute, Samuel Huston College, and Rust College before assuming the presidency of Clark. He served until 1939.

There's a school on a hill
That we love good and true,
With a love that enlightens
Our souls through and through.
'Tis the shrine of a race, and
'Tis owned by a King,
And dear to our hearts
Are the praises we sing.

Oh, we love every building
That stands on the hill,
And we love even the trees
Waving, whispering still.
And oft to our dear
Alma Mater we hark!
Oh, God bless you and keep you,
Our dear old Clark!

These are the words to the old Clark University's "Alma Mater," which was printed in the school's yearbook and journal, *The Mentor*.

Thirkield Hall was on the Gammon Theological Seminary campus at Capitol Avenue, about two miles from the State Capitol Building. The building included a chapel, lecture and classrooms, a museum, parlor and offices, as well as dormitory rooms.

The 1928 Clark Panthers football team was known as the Black Battalion of Death. They were the winners of the first Turkey Day game between Clark and Morris Brown on November 28, 1929, before a crowd of eight thousand fans at the Ponce de Leon Ballpark. The team was coached by Samuel Taylor from 1925 to 1931.

Leslie Baker, a graduate of Clark University, was also a member of the Omega Psi Phi basketball team, which was a part of the Interfraternity Basketball Council. He became football coach and later athletic director at Booker T. Washington High School. (Digging It Up Archives.)

Annie Lou Watters, a native of Rome, Georgia, graduated from Clark University in 1929. She received her Masters in Library Science and returned to Atlanta, where she became assistant librarian at the Auburn Branch of the Carnegie Library. She was later named head of the branch. (Mrs. Annie McPheeters.)

Thirteen

Morehouse College

This postcard view of the Morehouse College campus features Sale Hall, Graves Hall, and the president's residence during the decade of the 1920s. This decade characterized successful academic life, cultural events, student activities, and faculty growth, according to E.A. Jones, author of *Candle in the Dark—A History of Morehouse College*. During the twenties, the enrollment in all of the departments (Academy, College and School of Religion) averaged about 450 students. Many great scholars joined the faculty during this decade, including a young Benjamin E. Mays, who taught mathematics, psychology, and philosophy. The school began its annual Shakespearean plays, published the school paper *The Athenaeum*, and enjoyed musical renderings from Professor Kemper Harreld and the Glee Club and the orchestra, which often featured renowned concert artists such as Roland Hayes and pianist Hazel Harrison.

A significant achievement of Morehouse during this decade was the creation of the Atlanta School of Social Work, born in the sociology classrooms of Professor Gary Moore and conceived in the intense interest of the Hopes, especially Mrs. Lugenia Burns Hope, who had already founded the Neighborhood Union and was serving as its president. (Digging It Up Archives.)

Born poor in Augusta, Georgia, John Hope became the first black president of Morehouse College in 1906 after joining the faculty in 1898, when it was the Atlanta Baptist College. He attended Brown University, where he graduated in 1894. Hope returned to Morehouse in 1919 after serving in France with the National YMCA. Upon his return, the new science building was completed in 1920. Hope was also a vice-president for the Citizens Trust Bank. In 1929, he joined with President Florence M. Read of Spelman College and Myron Adams, president of Atlanta University, to establish the Atlanta University Center and became president of the new university. John Hope died in 1936. (Digging It Up Archives.)

Here, Dean Samuel Archer stands tall and stately on the grounds of his beloved Morehouse College. A native of Virginia, he graduated from Colgate University, where he was an outstanding athlete. He coached football at Morehouse from 1905 to 1908 and 1912 to 1915. From 1931 to 1937, he served as the fifth president of the school. Archer was very active in educational, social, and civic affairs in Atlanta and was a charter member of Kappa Boule of Sigma Pi Phi Fraternity. A high school was later named in his honor in the 1950s. (Digging It Up Archives.)

Pictured here are Coach Harvey and the 1924–1925 Morehouse football team.

The Morehouse College Homecoming Court was captured in this c. 1925 photograph. (Digging It Up Archives.)

The Morehouse College Orchestra was under the direction of a nationally known violinist and the head of the music departments of Morehouse and Spelman, Kemper Harreld. In addition to being director of the Glee Club, Professor Harreld provided musical lessons to many people and presented recitals throughout the city at local churches and other cultural events. He was also the vice-president of the National Association of Negro Musicians. (Digging It Up Archives.)

Morehouse offered an academy which featured grade level classes. These young boys were in the sixth grade at the academy in 1922. (Digging It Up Archives.)

The 1928–1929 Morehouse Basketball team was coached by B.T. Harvey and included Nelson T. Archer (front row, third from left), the tall and statuesque son of Dean Samuel Archer of Morehouse College. Nelson graduated with the Class of 1929 after a standout basketball career for the Maroon Tigers. (Digging It Up Archives.)

Graduating in the Morehouse College Class of 1929 was William Holmes Border (third row, second from right); Borders would become the pastor of Wheat Street Baptist Church on Auburn Avenue The commencement ceremony was held on Tuesday, June 4, in Sale Hall. It was in this class that sixteen men completed the academy. Morehouse also awarded degrees to six women: Alice Umestine Bell (the second wife of John Lewis, president of Morris Brown), Hannah Elizabeth Buchanan, Mary Emma Burney, Rebecca Dickerson, Florence Mae Harvey, and Tena Beatrice Maxey.

Shown here are the charter members of the Alpha Rho Chapter of Alpha Phi Alpha Fraternity at Morehouse College, c. 1924. By the 1920s, the school had chapters of four Greek letter fraternities. (Father H.J.C. Bowden.)

After completing the eighth grade in Montgomery, Alabama, T.M. Alexander (left) entered Morehouse Academy, the high school of Morehouse College. He completed his studies in 1927 and continued on in the college, participating in the Glee Club, orchestra, debate team, and Alpha Phi Alpha Fraternity. He graduated in 1931 and became one of the most successful entrepreneurs in Atlanta, establishing Alexander and Company, a full-time insurance agency. His life story is chronicled in his book *Beyond the Timberline*.

Fourteen

Morris Brown
University

" Haven For All Hungry Souls, Feeding them shall be thy goal."
Alma Mater

Founded in 1881, Morris Brown University was established by the African Methodist Episcopal Church in the basement of Big Bethel AME Church. By 1920, the campus had grown, and it offered elementary, high school, and normal schools, as well as a nursing school, a seminary, and satellite schools in Cuthbert and Savannah, Georgia. In Atlanta, the administration and classroom building (seen here) was located on the corner of Houston Street and Boulevard. Other buildings on the picturesque campus included Flipper Hall, a five-story brick building with fifty-eight-room boys dormitory. Wylie Hall was turned into a classroom building. In addition, the Fair Haven Hospital on Irwin Street was organized in 1916, during the administration of President Fountain. (Digging It Up Archives.)

John Lewis, a 1913 graduate of Yale University, was named president of Morris Brown College in 1920. He succeeded Rev. William A. Fountain, who was elected bishop. Lewis had been pastoring a church in California before assuming the presidency. During his administration, the school purchased the Boulevard Public School, which became the home of Turner Theological Seminary. The college enrollment also increased from seventy-five to two hundred students. President Lewis served until 1928, when he resigned due to lack of funds to support the school's programs and operational expenses. He would return to the presidency in 1950 and serve until his death in 1958. (Digging It Up Archives.)

The second-year class of Morris Brown College posed in front of the main building, c. 1921. The faculty of the school had talented instructors, including G.R. Hgginbotham (tailoring), Dean Wellington G. Alexander (School of Religion), Annie B. Thomas (history), Edward W. Browne (School of Commerce), Ruby Rose Drake (School of Education), and Willie F. McKinney (School of Music). (Digging It Up Archives.)

Five years after the Phi Beta Sigma Fraternity was founded in January 1914, at Howard University, the first chapter of the Phi Beta Sigma Fraternity in the South, the Zeta Chapter, was established at Morris Brown College during the fall of 1919. From this chapter came Walter M. Clarke, the first undergraduate to serve as president (1921–1922); R.O. Billings, future national president; Cornelius V. Troup, editor of the fraternity's journal *The Crescent*; and Charles Moore, national treasurer. The Conclave was held in Atlanta in 1921. Phi Beta Sigma brother George Washington Carver attended and spoke during the convention.

The Phi Beta Sigma Fraternity helped to establish the second chapter of Zeta Phi Beta Sorority, at Morris Brown University in 1921, the first sorority at a black college in Georgia. The charter members included Miss Eugenia F. Chiles (back row, fourth from right), who was second general president of the young national organization; and Miss Amelia Hall (back row, third from left), daughter of Rev. J.T. Hall (pastor of Big Bethel), who would go on to have a stellar career as a teacher and principal of the I.P. Reynolds School. The graduate chapter of the sorority, Epsilon Zeta Chapter, was established in 1923–24 by Alice Dugged Carey (back row, third from right). This photograph was taken *c.* 1921. (Digging It Up Archives.)

During the 1920s, the Morris Brown College Quartet featured Edward Mitchell (seated), dean of the college who would later serve as president of Morris Brown College. The director and pianist was Essie M. Groves. (Digging It Up Archives.)

The boys dormitory was named for Bishop Flipper.

Members of the Morris Brown College Football team of *c.* 1925 are pictured here. During the 1920s, the team was coached by T. Addison and Belford V. Lawson.

Bishop Joseph Simeon Flipper was chancellor of Morris Brown during the 1920s. Born in 1859, he attended the Storrs School on Houston Street and was one of the first students to enter Atlanta University. After a stint at teaching, he was licensed to preach in the AME church. Flipper served as dean of the theology department at Morris Brown and was later elected president of Morris Brown in 1904. Flipper's brother Henry was the first African American to attend West Point Academy.

A group of Spelman coeds posed in front of the Grover Werden Memorial Fountain, which was dedicated on May 31, 1927. Spelman hosted the annual conference of the Student YWCA with representatives from nine Southern states numbering over hundred students. (Digging It Up Archives.)

The *Campus Mirror*, a publication which featured news, poetry, and prose of Spelman, began in 1924. (Digging It Up Archives.)

Fifteen
Spelman College

Spelman entered the 1920s under the leadership of Lucy Hale Tapley, who served until 1927. Near her departure, Sisters Chapel was constructed in 1927, providing the largest auditorium facility for the Atlanta University schools. During her administration, many changes were made at the school. In 1924, Spelman Seminary was changed to Spelman College. The 1920s introduced the first Spelman Christmas concert in 1928. Several programs were discontinued, including the Elementary School and Nurses Training Department. McVicar Hospital was closed to outside patients. Margaret Nabrit Curry became the first African American on the faculty in 1925, Kemper Harreld was added to the music department in 1927, and Anne Cooke became director of drama in 1928. Other images relating to Spelman appear on the opposite page. (Digging It Up Archives.)

Spelman President Florence Read (center), who was appointed in 1927, is shown with John Hope (second from left) and other dignitaries, including James Weldon Johnson (third from right). Under the terms of the Atlanta University Center agreement, Spelman would retain its identity as a liberal arts college for women, Morehouse would serve in the same capacity for men, and Atlanta University would drop its undergraduate courses and develop graduate and professional departments. While the schools continued to use the old campus, a new campus site was soon selected and new buildings constructed. (Digging It Up Archives.)

Left: Griff Davis, a graduate of Morehouse College (shown with his wife, *c.* 1919), was superintendent of buildings and grounds at Spelman College.

Right: Three of the six daughters of John Wesley Dobbs are pictured here; from left to right are Willie, Josephine, and Irene in the yard of their home at 400 Houston Street, *c.* 1922. Irene was named valedictorian of her high school class at Spelman Laboratory High School in 1925. Her speech topic was "Harlem: The Center of Race Consciousness." She would become the mother of the future mayor of Atlanta, Maynard Jackson. All of the Dobbs girls graduated from Spelman College. Sisters not shown are Millicent, Mattiwilda, and June. (Josephine Dobbs Clement/Andre Vann.)

124

Epilogue

Marcus Garvey (far right), the "Black Ponzi" and founder of the Universal Negro Improvement Association, is shown observing one of the numerous parades of the association members. Garvey was extradited and imprisoned at the Federal Penitentiary in Atlanta in February of 1923, where he remained until November of 1927. (Herman Reese.)

Washington High School students developed musical interests under the talents of Graham Jackson, who joined the faculty in 1924 as director of vocal and instrumental music. Jackson had worked at the Paramount Theater on Auburn Avenue as a vaudeville performer and was enrolled at Morehouse College, *c.* 1925. (Digging It Up Archives.)

In December of 1929, the National Organization of Alpha Phi Alpha Fraternity held its 22nd General Convention in Atlanta, which featured three of the founders of the organization. The organization was founded in 1906 at Cornell University. During the convention, members of the Klu Klux Klan marched down Auburn Avenue to protest their convention. With a theme "Jim Crow Must Go," the Alphas helped Atlanta close out the decade of the twenties. (Digging It Up Archives.)

Roland Hayes, world-renowned tenor, appeared at the Atlanta Auditorium on December 18, 1925. He resided in the home of Dr. and Mrs. Charles H. Johnson. Chairing the welcoming committee were Mr. and Mrs. Kemper Harreld. Harreld was director of the Glee Club and orchestra at Morehouse College. (Digging It Up Archives.)

Acknowledgments

To God be the Glory for completion of another project. To Jim Dunn and the Arcadia Press family—is this a match made in heaven or what?

I am deeply indebted to many people who helped to make this and all my publications possible. First, the support of my mother, Deloris Hughes; father, Herman "Pop" Mason; and sisters, Dionne and Minyon; Dr.'s Lorene and Paul Brown; Robert and Kendra Nealy; Dorothy Nealy; Jacquelyne Burke; Geraldine and Walter Pritchett; Eva McLendon; and the Therrell High and Morris Brown families. Their support helps me to "dig up" images and research the text. My computer consultant and friend Patrick Stephens, you are godsend! A very special thank you to two of the greatest librarians the profession has produced, Casper Jordan and Ella Gaines Yates, for reading and editing the manuscript. I would like to acknowledge and thank the following persons for the loan of photographs or research assistance: Edward Bowen, who gave me a shopping bag full of his family's photos; Margaret Jacobs; Alice Holmes Washington; Emma Amos; the Herndon Foundation; Dr. Carole Merritt; the Apex Museum; the Auburn Avenue Research Library; Clara Yates Hayley, for the boxes of "stuff"); Clara Axam; Gladys Willingham and the Hanley Funeral Home; Isaiah "Ike" Blocker; Rev. Lewis Jay; Ed Cahill; the late Harry Murphy; Rose Martin Palmer; Jeanette Harvey Hamme; the Atlanta History Center; Morehouse College; the *Atlanta Journal and Constitution*; the *Atlanta Daily World*; Portia Scott; Ruth Simmons; Alexis Scott Reeves; Haroldeen Crowder; Dr. Asa Yancey; Harriet Nash Chisholm; the late Wynelle Hannon; George Rice; Walter "Billy" Reid; Lottie Heywood Watkins; the late Henry J.C. Bowden; Mamie Thomas; and Jenelsie Holloway. Special thanks to Andre Vann and Willis Jones, who are currently documenting the histories of their cities respectively. "This is our gift and our ministry, let us use it to glorify his name." Also, special thanks go Westside and St. James CME Churches.

Special thanks also to my "old gang" at the Auburn Avenue Research Library and Central branch: Janice Sikes, Gloria Mims, Sharon Robinson, Gloria Strong, and Joyce Jelks. Your continued and consistent support sustains me. To my nieces, another book for your future knowledge. Finally, one of the greatest resources in the city is the **Atlanta Independent and Atlanta Daily World Newspapers**. No history of Black Atlanta can be complete without using them. I could not have done this or any other book without them.

Finally, I am grateful for the long-standing support of Pamela Pryor Fuller, Kathleen Bertrand, Elliot Ferguson and the gang at the Atlanta Convention and Visitor Bureau, Ingrid Saunders Jones, Deborah Richardson Heard and Dr. Herman Reese, Maurice Jenkins, Clarence Johnson and Larry Epps, and the brothers of Eta Lambda Chapter of Alpha Phi Alpha Fraternity.

Bibliography

Alexander, T.M. *Beyond The Timberline: The Trials and Triumphs of a Black Entrepreneur.* Edgewood: M.E. Duncan and Co., 1992.

Buckely, Gail Lumet. *The Hornes: An American Family.* New York: Alfred A. Knopf, 1986.

Coleman, Gregory. *We're Heaven Bound: Portrait of a Sacred Drama.* Athens: University of Georgia Press, 1994.

Dittmer, John. *Black Georgia in the Progressive Era 1900–1920.* Urbana: University of Illinois Press, 1977.

Garrett, Franklin M. *Atlanta and Environs: A Chronicle of its Peoples and Events.* Atlanta, 1954.

Guy-Sheftall, Beverly. *Spelman: A Centennial Celebration.* Atlanta: Spelman College, 1981.

Henderson, Alexa Benson. *Atlanta Life Insurance Company: Guardian of Black Economic Dignity.* Tuscaloosa: University of Alabama Press.

Jones, Edward A. *A Candle in the Dark: A History of Morehouse College.* Valley Forge: Judson Press, 1967.

Kuhn, Clifford M., Harlon E. Joye, and E. Bernard West. *Living Atlanta: An Oral History of the City.* Atlanta: Atlanta Historical Society; Athens: University of Georgia Press, 1990.

Lewis, David Levering. *When Harlem Was in Vogue.* New York: Alfred A. Knopf, 1984.

Mason, Herman "Skip." *Going Against The Wind: A Pictorial History of African-Americans in Atlanta.* Atlanta: Longstreet Press, 1992.

Pomerantz, Gary M. *When Peachtree Meets Sweet Auburn: The Saga of Two Families and the Making of Atlanta.* New York: Lisa Drew/Scribner, 1996.

Sewell, George A. and Cornelius V. Troup. *Morris Brown College: The First Hundred Years.* Atlanta, 1981

Other Publications produced by Digging It Up, Inc.:
Auburn Avenue/Dobbs Plaza Historical Interpretive Program.
City of Decatur/DeKalb County African-American Historical Interpretive Project.
Atlanta University Center/West Side Historical Interpretive Program.
Mechanicsville: A Collection of Historical Data.

Other Publications used:
Sweet Auburn: The Thriving Hub of Black Atlanta by Alexa Henderson and Eugene Walker (M.L. King National Historic Site and Preservation District, 1984)
The Sweet Auburn Avenue Business History 1900–1988 by William L. Calloway.
Paper: "The Awakening of Black Political Power in Atlanta, 1900–1946" by Louis Williams, Ph.D. Prairie View A&M University.

About the Author: Skip Mason, a native of Atlanta, is a professor of history at Morehouse College and founder/president of Digging It Up, Inc. He is the author of several publications, including *Going Against the Wind: A Pictorial History of African-Americans in Atlanta*; *Hidden Treasures: Black Photographers in Atlanta*; *African-American Life in Jacksonville*; and *The Talented Tenth: The Seven Jewels of Alpha Phi Alpha Fraternity.*